AN ARCHAEOLOGY
OF YEARNING

AN ARCHAEOLOGY OF YEARNING

A MEMOIR BY
BRUCE MILLS

etruscan press

Etruscan Press
Wilkes University
84 West South Street
Wilkes-Barre, PA 18766
(570) 408-4546

www.etruscanpress.org

Published 2013 by Etruscan Press
Printed in the United States of America
Cover design by Michael Ress
Interior design and typesetting by Julianne Popovec
The text of this book is set in Minion Pro.

First Edition

13 14 15 16 17 5 4 3 2 1

Library of Congress Cataloguing-in-Publication Data

Mills, Bruce, 1958-
  An archaeology of yearning : a memoir / by Bruce Mills. -- First edition.
    pages cm
  1. Mills, Bruce, 1958---Biography. 2. Autistic children--Biography.
  3. Autistic children--Family relationships. 4. Fathers and sons--
  Biography. 5. Parents of autistic children--Psychology. I. Title.
  RJ506.A9M588 2013
  618.92'85882--dc23
                              2013019861

Please turn to the back of this book for a list of the sustaining funders of Etruscan Press.

For Mary, Sarah, and Jacob
and my parents, Herb and Elaine Mills

Archaeology is our voyage to the past, where we discover who we were and therefore who we are.

—Camilla Paglia

I must begin with an account of our starting point and recall and describe the first period, in order that the progress we have made may be better appreciated. By thus contrasting the past with the present, we can determine what ought to be expected from the future.

—Jean Marc Gaspard Itard

As long as you yearn, you can't congeal: there is a forward motion to yearning.

—Gail Godwin

An Archaeology of Yearning

ACKNOWLEDGMENTS

I have received support, large and small, from many people. At Kalamazoo College, I owe a special debt to Andy Mozina, whose close attention to the manuscript as a whole can be felt throughout the book. Along the way, Con Hilberry, Marion Hilberry, Jim VanSweden and Amy Smith provided timely reflections on early chapters. Through annual campus readings, Gail Griffin, Marin Heinritz, Amelia Katanski, Diane Seuss, and Babli Sinha voiced ongoing encouragement. As for those colleagues who have moved on, I thank Glenn Deutsch, Kathy Crown, Lisbeth Gant-Britton, and Ellen Caldwell for their feedback and faith in the writing.

Over the years, I have also drawn from conversations with many students in my first-year seminar, Autism and Other Ways of Knowing.

Both indirectly and directly, I have also been fortunate to see my work through the eyes of many writers who, for personal or professional reasons, have found themselves among those on the autism spectrum: Kristina Chew, Debra Cumberland, James Fisher, Vicki Forman, Mark Osteen, and Ralph Savarese. My book is richer for this re-seeing through their experiences and insights.

During my time at the Bread Loaf Writers' Conference as the B. Frank Vogel Scholar in Nonfiction, I benefited from the feedback of Garrett Hongo, Rus Bradburd, and my fellow nonfiction scholars, Fred Bahnson and Kimberly Meyers.

A special thanks as well to PJ Mark, who helped me get the manuscript into a shape more fitting for publication.

I gratefully acknowledge the previous venues for three pieces: "An Archaeology of Yearning," *The Georgia Review*; "Sleeping with Jacob," *New England Review;* and "The Meltdown," *Gravity Pulls You In: Perspectives on Parenting Children on the Autism Spectrum*. I am especially indebted to Stephen Donadio and Carolyn Kuebler at *NER* for their support.

To Philip Brady, executive editor at Etruscan Press, who enthusiastically embraced the book and to Starr Troup, managing editor, who clearly understood and effectively shepherded this project to its publication, I also owe deep thanks. You have helped complete a long journey.

Finally, I wish to acknowledge my daughter, Sarah, and partner, Mary, for their patience and love, and my son, Jacob, whose own love and rituals of living compel me to write and to reconsider all that I think I know.

AN ARCHAEOLOGY
OF YEARNING

I. *The Imaginary Grid*

FLESH AND BLOOD

Scientists speculate that one anatomical change—the development of the voice box, those tenuous strands tucked in our throat—precipitated that miraculous evolution to modern human. Even now I marvel at this budding stutter of muscles, this echo chamber of flesh and blood. I wonder at the deep yearnings that first exercised the throat and tongue, the vowels rounded out of some primal joy or pain. Cave paintings still remain dark and liminal compared with this taste of compressed air.

At night, Mary and I huddle together, the soft lamp light casting the shadows of our limbs upon the wall. We rehearse the events of the day, reserving a ritualistic place for the gentle word by word caress of our children's names and their naming. Sarah. Jacob. Without this word play, it seems, we would disappear half-formed into sleep.

We talk of Jacob. He has autism. If the evening was a difficult one, if he had only the vague gesture of language for meanings rich and intense in his mind, we find ourselves licking the blood of small crescent marks on our arms where he pinched us in frustration. "What is happening?" he cries when he kicks, when we will not let him watch another episode of "The Magic School Bus" or "Where in the World Is Carmen San Diego?" "What is happening? What is happening?" We know that we have heard these words before in some forgotten video or story. We wonder whether something important might be revealed if we found the source.

After I turn off the light, I recall images of day: the precise chorus line of animal figures, small to large, that Jacob has posed on the window bench; the tangle of Sarah and Jacob on the hardwood floor, watching the animated version of Tomie de Paola's children's book Bill and Pete; *Sarah's endless evening chatter; Jacob's incessant movement.*

Now here I am mixing words like red ochre in my hands, lining my sounds like cave art, caught up in my own private symbols. What is happening? What is this red on my tongue? What is the meaning of the blood on my wrist, the crescent moon of finger nails pressed hard to the flesh?

MYSTERIES

"Oh, l-ook. A nice dinna!"

Jacob looks past my eyes and points toward the top of the refrigerator. The end of his right index finger curls slightly downward, as if he knew himself that nothing is to be found amid the dusty tops of things.

"Oh, l-ook." His tongue holds the "l" as if a whole note; the "ook" forms a Dr. Seussian accompaniment. When I pick him up, he twists in my arms like a wild thing and grips the door jamb. We are a raft adrift. His arms are oars catching the sides of the river bank; we have no word for shore. The torque of this leaning pulls at my back, yet I still guide him forward until his hands find the refrigerator. He leaves the dots of his fingertips in the dust.

"What do you want, Jacob? Tell me what you want."

"Oh, l-ook. Oh, l-ook. A nice dinna!"

For Mary and me, the early years of autism were full of these inexplicable mysteries. I think of them as the wandering times, the wilderness days of storytelling in the face of the unpredictable and unknown. Family and friends lent their own memories because the new ones of Jacob did not fit our remembrances of Sarah's early development. Relatives recalled the uncle who sat mute among his siblings—and then chose to begin talking at four. Neighbors related the odd fixations of now gifted adults, musicians and artists who, like our son, seemed disinterested in chatter and the social life of jungle gyms. Sometimes, this remembering seemed to urge an unspoken moral: the good parent should not hover or fret with the child who does not chat. Eventually, confusion and doubt filled the spaces that opened up in the uncertainty. What if we did not attend properly to diet, to hints of developmental delays, to the need to intervene earlier in the face of his silence and sleepless nights? Was there something else we could have done or should have known? And then there were the irrational moments, the wondering whether some lack of faith or humility set these new mysteries in motion. What ignorance or arrogance led to this unexpected play and our helpless looking? In these unraveling seasons, a fine line existed between reason and superstition, between the stubborn belief in the miracles of self-denial and the self-evident facts of Jacob's withdrawal. Though we learned that autism affected communication and social interactions as well as manifested itself in unusual or intense fixations and rituals, we saw no clear path through the confusion of his peculiar phrasings and behaviors. As a result, I felt like a wanderer, the father in some fable who discovers a lost child, brings him into the home, and provides steaming soup and hand-me-down clothes—only to find that the orphan cannot speak or can only utter unfamiliar words. Our waking hours were filled with endless detective work to find the meaning behind private codes and gestures.

Sometimes we knew how to solve the mysteries. One Saturday afternoon, we were on the back deck, talking with our friends, Marion and Con. Jacob came out with a pair of scissors, a long, hot dog-shaped balloon that we had blown up earlier in the day, and a red scrap of construction paper.

"Red udder," he said, urgently handing me the items.

He was around six, had been diagnosed with autism at three, and so we had learned a disciplined patience in the face of his sudden requests.

"Red udder. Red udder."

The balloon skidded atop the table, its rubbery smell sticking to my fingers as I thumped it rhythmically against my forearm. We all looked at each other, perplexed. Jacob took the red construction paper and held it against an end of the balloon. For a moment, I remembered not to think with words; I emptied my mind of the clutter of questions and did not panic at his enigmatic phrase.

Ruminating on the long tube of the balloon and the red slip of paper hanging at its bottom, I glimpsed the answer. It came to me in color, like a quick glance at an impressionist painting of an autumn tree, leaves just splotches or dots of red, auburn, and rust. I saw the tube as a metal cylinder rising toward the stars atop a fiery burst. A rocket. He wanted me to make a rocket ship.

"Rocket ship," I said, pleased to have the words to give to my son and relieved to have avoided an afternoon of his fretful, roving efforts to be understood. Jacob took in a deep breath and let his arms rest upon Mary's lap. His leaning was relaxed, though his eyes still intently watched my cutting.

"'Rocket,' say 'rocket,' Jacob." He was not paying attention, of course. "Red udder" had communicated his want.

As I cut and taped, I wondered what chance combination of memories enabled me to translate his words, this image voiced in sparse vowels and consonants. And then my thoughts wandered back to the associations that had flashed in my mind. I realized that what he wanted came to me when I caught an image of a nursery rhyme. During the past week, we had been reading from a book of Mother Goose rhymes, including the one about the cow jumping over the moon. I went down to the basement to get the book. Against the backdrop of a night sky, I saw that white cow, udder hanging over the curve of the moon as the blocky body seemed to lift off toward outer space. I needed the story-rhyme to call out the proper scene, the one that Jacob imagined and translated into hieroglyphic speech.

There is another tale, one that I pondered again and again in those wilderness years: the Exodus story in the Old Testament. It held the kind of images and associations that contributed to my own sense of what was happening, my own internal meaning-making. The story was linked to the name that Mary and I first considered for a boy child but then later discarded like a scrap of paper: Aaron, the brother of Moses. In the splintered remembrances of the Exodus story, I recalled the various desires that come with trying to escape or striving to conjure up faith to confront the unknown.

I had always been drawn to Aaron in the Bible story. It may be that the attraction arose from watching *The Ten Commandments*, the Hollywood film that recreates the Israelites' flight from Egypt through the Red Sea. The biblical story contains its own cinematic and dramatic texture, including the ultimate fear of having been chosen by God without the confidence or ability to carry out His commands. When it is revealed that he has been selected to lead the Israelites out of slavery to the Promised Land, Moses timidly tries to convince his God that he should not be sent; he worries about his own ineloquence:

> "If you please, Lord," he beckons, "I have never been eloquent, neither in the past, nor recently, nor now that you have spoken to your servant; but I am slow in speech and tongue."
>
> But the Lord said to him, "Who gives one man speech and makes another deaf and dumb? . . . Is it not I, the Lord? Go, then! It is I who will assist you in speaking and will teach you what you are to say."

Yet Moses still insists that someone else be chosen, that he has not the power to carry the word to his people. In anger, Yahweh replies:

> "Have you not your brother, Aaron the Levite? I know that he is an eloquent speaker.... You are to speak to him, then, and put the words in his mouth. I will assist both you and him in speaking and will teach the two of you what you are to do."

Perhaps, in those early years, my desire to reflect upon this story is not surprising. After all, I had begun to grieve for a lost son, a child I had seen in my mind's eye but had not embraced in life. In my private storytelling, the imaginings that prefaced Jacob's birth repeatedly called forth the image of the eloquent one, the progeny who could take a lost people across their own Jordan River to some better place. With both my daughter and son, in fact, I had done as many parents do: I had pictured the embodiment of the best of who

I was or the best of what I could nurture in my future children's lives. In these prophetic hopes and reveries, it was my love that shaped their eloquent leadership. Then came these irrational questions: Was this the arrogance that left me unprepared? Was it this turning to earthly desires that initiated the hard years? How easy it was to slip into these superstitious doubts to give order to what I did not understand.

But I can say now what I was just coming to know then in a house resounding with the Jabberwock of Jacob-speak: that to be chosen is to be sacrificed and that to be sacrificed is to come to a new way of knowing. Something unsustainable had to be given up; something new had to be discovered. And it was the story of Moses and Aaron that crystallized this understanding. What a bitter lesson to find oneself delivered into a wilderness, to set up camp there, to tend the fire and suffer the endless covering of coal and ash, to feel the grind of sand in the unleavened bread, to embrace the initial certainty of false gods, to see the distant shadow that starts as Jordan and ends in a bitter stream of cursing. The most holy of mysteries is this very human place, this shoreline defining the tenuous threshold between sacrifice and deliverance, confusion and faith.

Near the time of looking back to this story, this reflection upon forsaken names, I unexpectedly wandered into a lesser, unsolved mystery: Jacob's puzzling, "Oh, l-ook. Oh, l-ook. A nice dinna." The unearthing of the phrase's origin came from entering another story plotted near the shores of the Nile, another tale that ended in the struggle to escape: Tomie de Paola's children's story, *Bill and Pete*.

After a day of cleaning, I sat down with Mary, Sarah, and Jacob (then eight and six) to watch a videotape of our family taken a number of years before. The television lit up with the image of my daughter and son, each four years younger, sitting on the living room floor. Their eyes were fixed upon an animated version of *Bill and Pete*. Bill is William Everett Crocodile, who lives on the banks of the River Nile. Pete is his toothbrush, that is, a bird that picks at Bill's molars beneath the canopy of the reptile's yawning jaws. When

William is young, he gets confused by all the letters required to spell his name. Pete unburdens him with the simple appellation, "Bill."

That night, I decided to read de Paola's story, and, after a period of searching, I caught a glimpse of the pink paperback with the moon and stars calm and steady on the back cover. As Jacob lined up dominoes on the floor next to his bed, I narrated the tale in the face of his seeming inattention until I came to the part I liked best. For my own amusement, I renamed Bill and Pete, Jacob and Dad. It was always fun to enter the stories destined to end in sleep or discovery. And I read:

> One Saturday, when there was no school, Jacob and Dad went down to the River Nile and sat on the bank in the sun. A man on a bicycle went riding by.
>
> Behind the bicycle were cages filled with crocodiles.
>
> "I wonder what that's all about?" said Jacob.
>
> "That's the Bad Guy, and those crocodiles are on their way to Cairo—to become suitcases," said an old crocodile swimming by. "Watch out he doesn't catch you!"
>
> But he did. The very next Saturday.
>
> Jacob and Dad were fishing and they didn't hear the Bad Guy creep up behind them.

For a moment, I saw my son pause and so I eased myself into the space of his play. On the rug, he had arranged dominoes in parallel lines. Squinting or with a quick or sidewise glance, I began to see the lines as credits scrolling upwards on a television or movie screen. I laid the book at the right edge of the dominoes and looked at the lines. In their configuration, I could almost see the words imprinted in his mind: the list of characters and voice credits, of executive producers, art directors, production assistants, gophers, hair stylists. From the black dots and black lines between the dots emerged the symbols of his world, a world of repetition, of rituals fulfilling needs that I had yet to understand. I quietly nudged the book against his elbow and, to draw his eyes to it, ran my finger along the golden shore that formed the border between palm trees and the blue water of the Nile. I began to read with more feeling.

The Bad Guy lassoed Jacob and put him in a cage. He didn't
pay any attention to Dad.
Dad tried to peck the Bad Guy, but Dad was just too small.
Poor Jacob!
He was on his way to Cairo.
All he could think about was suitcases.
Brave Dad!
He stayed close to his son.
The Bad Guy put Jacob in his garden and went into the house.
"Run me a nice hot tub, Jeeves," the Bad Guy said to his butler.
"I will take a bath before dinner. I got me another crocodile today
and I need a nap. Call me when the bath is ready."
"Tomorrow that crocodile becomes a suitcase," he added.

I narrated Dad's courage, how he picked the lock with his beak
and urged Jacob to escape quickly from the dangers of this cruel
man. But Jacob would not leave. He wanted to prevent the Bad Guy
from catching more crocodiles and creating more suitcases. So, the
crocodile slipped into the bathtub, his head barely visible near the
rubber ducky, and chased the villain out into the night.

I squeaked like the rubber ducky on Sesame Street and, following this train of thought, squeezed the airy laugh of Ernie through
my tongue and the roof of my mouth. Jacob swung his hand at my
face, trying to stop my imitation by hitting me. I rolled away from
the arch of his swinging hand, letting the pages crest in the air before
flattening on the floor. For a moment, I rubbed Jacob's back; I said,
"Dad stop" to reassure him. And then, after my son attended again to
the dominoes, I opened the book, turning from the backside of the
Bad Guy to the next page, to the image of Jacob and Dad (that is, Bill
and Pete) standing beside a dinner table. In the silence, I heard these
words escape from my tongue:
"Oh, look, a nice dinner," said Dad.
"And am I hungry," said Jacob.
It took a moment to awaken to the resonance of these lines, to
overlay Jacob's past utterances upon the original text. "Oh, l-ook, oh,
l-ook," I heard, "Oh, l-ook, a nice dinna."

Later, after I tucked Jacob in and promised to come back to sleep with him, I sat at the top of the stairs and wept. For years, I had not done so, had not let myself slip into this kind of grief. I wept because I had glimpsed what might have been Jacob's distant loneliness, his wanting to know that another person in the intimate world of our home knew where his imagination had gone. I cried for the urgency of my son's articulate yearning and for my own unknowing.

I still continue to read the moment like a sacred text. Were his words about hunger, not the kind that marks the emptiness in the stomach but that gives voice to the chaos of not being understood? Could it have been as simple as needing to hear me say the next line, as wanting a response to an anxious call, the assurance of a shared picture book and fixed storyline to confront an apprehension that arises in a world of ever-changing scripts?

Of course, it could mean many, many things. At the time when he had begun to lose language, when physical gestures had taken over where words had existed, Jacob could have found an emotional affinity with these lines. His mind could have woven the tone and color into some meaning to which he only had access—but sought to share. To his young ears and eyes, did the slapstick of the Bad Guy capture the dangers of adult whims and warnings? (And did Bill's cage and Pete's urgent pecking at the lock lead to the worrisome tone of Jacob's echolalia?) Even words meant to name what has passed or to point toward the present feast can carry worry. Their exodus is a reminder of the place where even God cannot be named, where the words that come tell of the need to slaughter the lamb and shut the door, where the passage to freedom runs the muddy gauntlet of the Red Sea, where the banks of the path rise like cresting waves. How should I hear his words? Were they a sign of a feast prepared, a banquet set for those who have endured years of slavery? Or a prophecy of famine, a slave's straw mat spread with the last of the unleavened bread?

I climb the stairs to find the book and look again at the last page. Even now, in a remembering that pulls at my chest, I feel a tightness, the expiration of breath in the body memory of a distant confusion.

There stands Bill with that silly, toothy grin suspended above the table. Just beneath Pete's beak rises the steam from what appears to be a bowl of rice or mashed potatoes. To the left, the Bad Guy streaks disrobed through the desert night. Above the feast, a yellow slice of moon smiles amid the blue.

And the stars, I want to say they seem to fall from the sky like manna; I want to say that they flew like doves back to Noah's ark. I want to see signs of passing things, of what has been and not what will be endured. No hunger. No apocalypse of water. But, in the outlines of this tale's beginning, I am still caught up in the young father's grieving, his struggling to make out the meaning of Jacob's words. I feel in my gut that distant time and place. It is as if I am the last of the chosen scrambling toward the distant shore. I hear the merciless thunder of the collapsing waves amid the cries of the faithless and know that I have surely lost my way.

Sleeping with Jacob

Since just after midnight, Jacob has been awake. He is nine. He wants Ludwig Bemelmans' Madeline to come out of the television. He extends his arm, makes straining noises, and acts as if he is reaching toward and into the TV downstairs. Hanging from a string taped to the slanting wall above our heads waves a drawing of Madeline. She is in a cloud. It is the kind of cloud that often leads from the mouths of comic strip characters, and I wonder if Jacob means for us to know that Madeline is in his dreams. I remind Jacob that Madeline is pretend, a storybook character. His body tightens at the news.

"Not pretend!" he says. "Reach. Reach. Not say pretend."

Tonight, Jacob is fighting something. After midnight, half-asleep, he kicked off the blankets and then pounded his feet against the wall and then against me.

For a short time, I try to relax. I know that it is likely Jacob will be awake all night or fall asleep shortly before dawn. Around the room, the signs of his demands begin to break out of the shadows: the red plaid sheet hanging from the curtain rods to keep out the morning light, the run of thin rope from bookshelves to ends of curtain rods that used to hold up sheets for a tent, two Madeline video boxes, scattered drawings of Madeline and Pepito, a Pooh helium balloon that dances against the ceiling when the heater kicks in. Beside me, Jacob asks repeatedly for Madeline. I stop answering, and he tosses his water cup across the room, tears off the bedding, and then lunges at me, pinching and scratching at my forearms. When he starts to throw books toward the window, I move in to hold him, wrapping my arms around his. Our feet shuffle in an awkward dance before we collapse to the floor. The room grows close with the smell of sweat and anger; my limbs ache with hopelessness.

Not every night is such a struggle. Jacob frequently sleeps from nine to six without interruption. Awake, he often lies wide-eyed but quiet, occasionally laughing or running through his own version of a video script or leaning toward me and uttering "hug." In time, he allows me to fall in and out of sleep. In the slumber broken occasionally by his sudden laughs and phrasings, I begin to imagine stories that I might tell. Beyond the red sheet and window blind, I think, moonlight washes the south side of the house. Toward the east, past the thick branches of an oak and the sullen stillness of its leaves, the stars begin to congregate. In this tale, I imagine the precarious dots of light mapping the constellation of our limbs, as if creating an enchanted blessing to redeem the day. On some nights, caught up in the promise of an image or combination of words as I edge toward sleep, I reach toward the floor to find something that might serve as a morning sign, something to help me remember where my story left off. I take whatever is within reach—a book or scrap of paper—and put it beneath my pillow or slide it toward an uncluttered space between bed and door. I am Hansel in the forest, hoping to leave just enough stones or bread crumbs to find the way back. More truthfully, Jacob is the forsaken child, and I am the father after his return. I yearn for the treasure taken after the witch's burning, the pearls that drive away hunger, the forgiveness of open hands and pockets emptied out. I want forgetfulness, no word of my anger, no hint of abandonment. My wants are abundant, thick as the needles beneath rows of pine.

Here is one memory stone near the open door. When I was younger, I used to tell Grimms' stories to my brother. He was nearly four, I was thirteen, and we both shared the same bedroom. In large families, it is rare that a child sleeps in a room or bed alone. For all of their years prior to high school, my sisters, three years apart, slept in the same bed. Until I was a sophomore (and my two older brothers had moved away), we rotated three single beds in a variety of arrangements.

In the first home that I can remember, we all slept in the narrow second-floor room of our small cape cod. After we moved, I was for a short time in the same room as my second oldest brother. When my first of two younger brothers came along ten years later, I soon became the older sibling sharing a room and occasional stories with the younger.

When I began the fairy tale of Hansel and Gretel from memory, I did not yet understand that bedtime stories fraught with evil risked restlessness and worked against the task at hand: ushering a child to sleep. Even now, I still feel the gut check of the sudden suspicion that the impending cruelty might be too much for my brother. I remember moving past the wickedness of the stepmother and the cowardice of the father; I lingered instead upon the ingenuity and wit of Hansel's effort to leave a trail and the magical features of the gingerbread house. I congratulated Gretel for her bravery and overlooked the oven's flames and witch's shrieks. With the ending, I painted a joyous reunion. (Looking over Grimms' published story, I realize that I had also forgotten much, including the jewels retrieved from the old woman's gingerbread house.) Perhaps I even invented a kind mother and left my brother imagining Hansel's and Gretel's full stomachs, warm beds, and forgetful slumber. But of all that comes back to me in the traces of this memory, I am still surprised by the vivid emotional echo of the storyteller's dilemma, the sudden worry of unleashing first-time fears like evils from Pandora's Box.

My grandmother also used to tell my older brothers, sisters, and me Grimms' tales. My father's mother lived in a small cottage on the east side of Storm Lake, the side that caught the snow blown across the ice during long Iowa winters and left six to ten foot drifts between homes. Bitter winds made her windows moan and whine in mid-January. In the spring, big-leafed rhubarb bordered her back yard, and in the damp, shady places beneath bushes and trees, a strong aroma of weedy flowers invaded the air. Inside, the small kitchen smelled of tea and cinnamon, the cupboard always seeming to hoard a pan of bread or graham cracker pudding atop wax paper. I learned to love the texture of soft foods like bread pudding with raisins, covered in thick cream. At some point during our visits, in the time after outside exploring and before our mother picked us up, my grandmother would sit us beside her on the couch or alongside a chair capped with cross-stitched doilies and tell stories. In these years, I heard "Hansel and Gretel" but also another Grimms' tale, "The Straw, the Coal, and the Bean." Spiced with a Liverpool accent, so exotic to the ear of an untraveled, midwestern boy, my British grandma told this brief tale of a precarious camaraderie forged after a chance escape from an old village woman's fire place and cooking pot. In the fragments of my remembering, I catch my innocent lingering upon the lesson of self-sacrifice: the thin straw's willingness to lay his body across a stream to allow for his friends' escape.

Curious to hear again this favorite story and to read the full version of "Hansel and Gretel," I tracked down an edition of Grimms' *Children's Stories and Household Tales.* In addition to reading of the redemptive reunion between the father and his children, of the jewels and precious stones, I learned that Straw did not experience a happy ending. Rushing upon his thin comrade as he lay stretched and hopeful across the brook, the hot-headed Coal paused fearfully when hearing the water below and burned Straw in half. Both plunged to death in the brook. Bean, having held back, burst his seam laughing and was later stitched back together. So, after all these years, why did I hold on so tenaciously to the moral of self-sacrifice? Had my grandmother altered the ending to soften its harshness? Did she field the inevitable questions of her grandchildren in ways that eased the hardness or uplifted the heroism? What would it have meant, after all, to imagine Straw's sacrifice as no more than a prelude to a meaningless fall or mocking laughter? As my grandmother looked into my eyes, she might have seen a child's need to believe in the possibility of such sacrifice; perhaps she knew that the story told only a partial truth, that it had forsaken goodness in the midst of evil, that death had erased Straw's generous impulse. So much, after all, can occupy that imaginative space. What should we remember and who should we praise: selfish Coal, cautious and unsympathetic Bean, or self-sacrificing Straw?

All storytellers face the problem of just how much to tell and just how to tell it. How much should be left out or let in? How piercing should the teller paint the evils of the world? How much of the tale changes in what the listener can understand and what the storyteller knows can be told at any given time?

My curious journeying back to Jacob and Wilhelm Grimm's book made me wonder how they wrestled with such questions and whether they spoke of this tale-teller's dilemma. Having listened to, recorded, and revised the hard-edged narratives, they must have considered, like any father sitting in the storyteller's chair or on the bed's edge, how they opened a world of fear and abandonment within the sanctuary of a family's sleeping quarters. In reading their preface to the second volume of the tales' first edition, we hear them express such a concern. "There are those," they write, "who do not even want [their children] to hear bad things about the devil" and parents who "might not want to put the book into the hands of their children." But, not surprisingly, they err on the side of the telling, concluding that they "do not know of a single healthy and powerful book used to educate the people (and that includes the Bible) in which such delicate matters do not actually appear to an even greater extent." In the folk tales, they see a "document of our hearts." If so, for both the storyteller and the listener, the document is of a kind that haunts as it heals. The stories that keep calling us back are also the ones that may keep us up at night.

In my years of learning about stories and how to read them, I remember once coming across the name of Bruno Bettelheim in relation to fairy tales, and so, in my library browsing, I sought out where this recollection might lead. Just as my grandmother sought to frame how to read Grimms' tales, Bettelheim must also have offered some insight into the stories. How might he illuminate these tales of famine, estrangement, and loss in the intimate home of memory and desire? Sitting down with *The Uses of Enchantment: The Meaning and Importance of Fairy Tales*, published in 1976, the same time as my bedtime storytelling to my brother, I read of Bettelheim's fascination with the harsh realities of Grimms' fairy tales and their important role in educating children. The hard facts represented in literature and especially fairy tales, Bettelheim cajoled readers, stimulate and enrich children's imaginations and consequently their developing minds and emotions. Seeing the world through a Freudian lens—and the psychoanalytical bogeymen of unconscious desires, "oedipal dilemmas," and "sibling rivalries"—he emphasizes the significance of Grimms' stories in the growth of identity and self-worth. To deal with inner tribulations and achieve self-understanding, children must engage in dream and fantasy: "[A child] can achieve this understanding, and with it the ability to cope, not through rational comprehension of the nature and content of his unconscious, but by becoming familiar with it through spinning out daydreams—ruminating, rearranging, and fantasizing about suitable story elements in response to unconscious pressures." In this way, it seems, self-understanding is not possible without stories and storytelling. We often make use of the short time before sleep to narrate the day in the context of near and far off fears.

It is not a bad thing, then, for parents and teachers to encourage children to sleep with all that might lead to sleeplessness. In important ways, a listener's unscripted fears and chaotic fantasies can be given shape through such troubling narratives as "Hansel and Gretel." With this kind of tough love, Bettelheim rejects what he sees as the widespread cultural desire to pretend that the "dark side of man does not exist" and asserts that "only by struggling courageously against what seem like overwhelming odds can man succeed in wringing meaning out of his existence." In the 1970s, *The Uses of Enchantment* must have seemed timely, an odd solace in the face of the era's violence within and beyond the nation, of alienated sons and daughters, of disillusioned citizens attempting to "wring meaning" from so much that was falling apart. Having survived time in a German concentration camp and yet still able to articulate the prospect of courage, compassion, and hope, Bettelheim himself seemed the storyteller to meet a parent's (and nation's) needs. He promised the possibility of mastering the evil within by doing more than simply offering the stories; he provided a master narrative, a way to piece together all the fragments: the mother's deception, the father's abandonment, and the child's exile or silence.

Still, caught up in these fantasies of psychoanalysis, I did wonder just how much to trust Bettelheim's shaping of Grimms' tales. Within the forest of his own enchanting logic, I began to lose what it meant to live with and in a tale, to sit beside the child, to taste the words as they drifted amid the smells of steaming tea and scones. I felt the imposition of meaning and a kind of forgetfulness, as if such stories do not shift and bend within the realities of an intimate storytelling. Is it not possible for the loving gesture, the timely sacrifice, to hold the weight of both suffering and hope and thus repair some painful gap or fracture in life? With her grandchildren upon her lap, my grandmother did not use her hands or words to choke meaning from a harsh world; she was no witch mixing evil with sweet breads. But, she did invite evil in, gradually, describing the outlines of wickedness and sorrow, letting our bodies lean against hers in the fear of the imagining. In this space, death did not go away; Straw and Coal still fell voiceless in the rushing stream. And, yet, having experienced a kind of exile from her home in leaving her family to come to the United States with her World War I husband, my grandmother must have known that the texture of a story's truth emerged in more than the hard and ever-present reality of loss. With some nudging, she invited a simultaneous and complicated truth—that the meaning changed with Straw's gesture, even when considered in light of the perhaps predictable rashness of Coal. In the legacy of this interpretation of the story, I find different questions. Is there an account of the tale where the bridge holds, where one can feel the heat scarring the back yet lie without breaking across the chasm? Or, perhaps, is the story of the falling just the beginning, a point where the listener takes up the emptiness without forsaking the need to cross the gap together?

I think of my son's restless nights and our wrestling in the dark. I recall the days and weeks when I felt the fall and the splash, felt his fingers in my flesh and my too-hard gripping of his body. But, if the truth be told, there is more in the remembering: the echo of "hug" and a leaning of his body into mine, a laughter and lightness of spirit that sees Madeline floating and shapes a world through the happy endings of Pooh. Can I find a way to capture the whole story? Can I see that at different times Jacob and I exchange the putting of our bodies down, the stretching toward the other side? Can I write a new story out of the old ways of seeing, a tale that honors the fall but holds more than death and loss?

Perhaps these questions point to the truth that another reader of Bettelheim, Maria Tatar, so eloquently expresses in *Off with Their Heads!: Fairy Tales and the Culture of Childhood*, a book that stood near *The Uses of Enchantment* on the library shelf: "Just as every rewriting of a tale is an interpretation, so every interpretation is a rewriting." Here, then, is one more framing of the storyteller's dilemma. In the end, no tale receives a passive listening; no telling enacts an innocent repeating. We can never get out of our place in the plot.

So what is my place in the tale? How can it be told? How does the imagination embrace the child or parent lost along some journey? How do the mother and father bargain for the son or daughter who has bitten from some forbidden fruit? Like children, adults, too, spin out their own fantasies.

Mary and I started sleeping with Jacob when he was five years old. He had always been a restless sleeper, unlike our daughter Sarah who, at six weeks, began sleeping through the night. We could not count on our son for such accommodation. Having learned to walk by nine months, Jacob soon mastered the gymnastics of climbing from his crib. It took a few weeks before we realized that he was spending parts of the night wandering in his room. When Mary or I brought him into our bed and laid him between us, he would rarely return to sleep. In the end, one of us would take him back to his room and nod off in the rocker or on the floor with Jacob looking on. Finally, succumbing to our need for sleep, we bought him a full-sized bed, cleared the room of any thing that might fall or be swallowed, and attached an outer latch to the door.

But nearing three years of age, he also began waking in a panic. When we arrived in his room, he would be shaking. It was as if the bedroom filled up with what he could not name, though once or twice, in his limited speech, he seemed to describe animal sounds or shapes. It was a panic that could not be calmed, could not be quickly soothed from his memory. What experiences or stories, we asked each other, haunted him to the point of such fear? Rocking with him, we would repeat, "It's all right; it's okay," and soon Jacob began to take up the incantation. "It's all right; it's okay," he would say, as we laid him back down, his limbs still trembling. We wondered why he would not call out our names when he needed us—and then we realized that he had rarely called us by name. And we thought of those nightmares from which we awake, gasping for air, unable to find our voices or words to cry out in recognition or for comfort. After we found out that Jacob had autism, we tried to remember that ignorance, not cruelty, had led us to abandon him in his trembling and wakefulness.

Sleeping with Jacob started slowly, the way hunger creeps up after a missed meal. We first tried the routines and rituals of our own childhoods; we read books, turned on the soft light of the night light, and rested against the bed until Jacob fell asleep. We picked out the stories composed for such times: *Goodnight Moon*, *Where the Wild Things Are*, *Weird Parents*. Eventually we brought up a single mattress to rest upon as we watched for signs of Jacob's slumber. It was more comfortable as we waited, though we often slipped into sleep before he did. Soon, we crawled into bed alongside our son and stayed through the night. We alternated nights, Mary usually sleeping four days of the week or five if my teaching schedule intensified. We stayed for five years.

Succumbing to such sleep fulfilled the needs that come with confusion and uncertainty. The evening began to seem more peaceful without the worry of Jacob's noises and aloneness. Moreover, when Mary or I slept with our son, we believed, in the better times, that it was a kind of gift, a brief respite for the other. We began to feel as if we had some control over or achieved some deliverance from the evils of the day: the after-school tantrums, the seemingly impossible diet recipes designed to "recover" our son, the uncertainties of medication, the urgent demands of work, the isolation from friends and family. Let loose during the daytime, the evils retreated at night—or so we pretended. Like all the stories that we told, we believed that our own wit and will, mixed with the sacrificial magic of sleepless love, could replenish and sustain us.

When I married, I thought that I would never again sleep alone. I knew that Mary and I would be apart at some time. She or I would return alone to family in Iowa or travel to a conference or workshop or interview. Still, with the exception of these infrequent absences, I pictured our bed as a place where the day ended—in conversation, in weariness, in making love, in the quiet play of what we knew and still wished to discover about who we were and wanted to be.

In marriage, this kind of knowing is its own story; it is the mystery that holds together the gaps in history and memory and motivates the desire that pervades the telling. It is a narration without resolution, however, for the past is endless and forever calls the other to ask and wonder and at times forgive. For instance, not long after we were married, I discovered a picture of my wife when she was twenty. She sits on a metal folding chair in her parents' basement. Behind her, the cement block wall gives greater distinctness to her white cotton shirt and red pants. Her left leg is crossed upon her right knee; her hands cup her left calf. She is unaware of the picture-taker. She looks toward a place that I cannot see; it is not in the room but something interior—perhaps something fleeting like a thought about driving home from college or perhaps something deep and intimate like a future child or a parent's death. So much history registers in this random flash. In looking upon this moment, this distant glance, I risk a kind of disorientation, a loss of bearings. How is it that, in our storytelling, we can act as if the unknown past and future can be taken in? How can I hope to knit together what seems so vast and unknowable? Yet, in first telling, I believe in the possibility of knowing, of holding together so much of the unwitnessed, of what has been and will be. In first embraces, after all, so much must be taken on faith. It is a faith that calls us toward the parts that have been left out or have yet to come. To get to these places, we must ask the unexpected question and develop the discipline of listening, of letting the mind's eye estrange the familiar.

Did the husband and wife in the tale of Hansel and Gretel begin with such desires? In the first days, at the edge of the imposing forest, the cottage might have seemed like a sanctuary. During the waking hours, the echo of the woodcutter's axe would have provided a reassuring cadence; for the wife, the mixing of flour, yeast, and water, the kneading of the dough, and the firing of the oven would not have yet become a burden. All might have been the taste of new seasonings, the replenishing moment spilling forth without hesitation. The deepest hunger must have been the desire that came from waiting, the yearning for the next disrobing, the taste of the remembering and telling, and the touch of tongue and breath. In the time of first knowing, this coming together might have been enough, this willingness to talk about the past without judgment or blame amid the fragrance of bread and pine sap.

What is it that was forsaken? What is it that could not sustain the possibility of imagining a way through the famine? The old story does not flesh out what must have been endured. That it was famine which broke the covenant seems the surest of truths. Famine is the slowest of tragedies. It may first come in hints, like happenstance and rumor. The rain does not fall; the blight speckles the first leaves. The neighbor's front door swings indifferently in the wind; the hoe leans unattended. The people left behind accommodate less. They learn that leanness can even be a mark of strength, the legacy of hard work and diligence. Hope and endurance give way to unsteadiness and malaise. Soon loss narrows into habits of survival; the mouth accepts coarse grain, not flour and bread, then chaff not wheat, then the unimaginable.

It is hard to look back at so many years attending so closely to so little. In my own world of work and home, I became an expert with rationing. As a teacher, I often paused during the day to multiply the number of student papers by the amount of time needed to read, compose responses, and record grades. The reading itself required a kind of empathy, a willingness to listen without intruding too quickly with judgment and correction. It demanded rest and, if rest was not possible, a willed attentiveness. Incoming sets of papers often meant between twenty to thirty hours of additional work over ten days—and then the next set of writing came in, and then the next. In one eleven-week semester, when committee and teaching responsibilities were especially burdensome, I would set the alarm for 3 am and fall asleep after I put my daughter to bed at 9 pm. Beside me, where Mary used to sleep, I left open the unfinished papers or chapters. I stemmed the chaos with numbers; I survived because I knew an end would come. The cycle of work guaranteed completion.

At times, I thought of what could be worse. I remembered the years when I contracted to detassel corn in the fields surrounding Storm Lake. In the summers during college, I would paint houses or farm buildings during the day and, in August evenings and weekends, make extra money by heading out to the fields. Once, my contract included half miles rows, i.e., pulling corn tassels from over six foot stalks, eight to ten inches apart, for a distance of a half mile. It took an hour and a half for one row. Doing this work required a mental discipline, a breaking down the ninety minutes into manageable units. Daydreaming was costly, though inevitable and calming.

In my own way, I unknowingly reduced mystery and story to a spread sheet. I only had so much to budget, literally, for my time at home. What, then, was the cost of a week of daily tantrums, holding Jacob's arms during his daytime meltdowns while Sarah sat on the stairs and cried or retreated to the basement? How much future interest should Mary and I forsake? We had our time. We had told enough personal histories to provide for the next month and year. Without clearly voicing the change, I began the hard bargain of survival. At night, after Mary left for bed, I slept because I could not stay awake and then awoke because it was necessary. My most productive work emerged in the dark mist of forgetfulness. I learned that story and memory are not like grain to be stored in the Pharaoh's bins and parceled out during lean times. Memory is a fluid thing, full of feeling and open doors. During the famine, it can be a wolf at the threshold, ready to devour the last of flesh and bone.

In the chaos that provides the stuff of life and fairy tales, evil and good sometimes knock with the same soft touch. When we open the door, we have only what we can imagine and generate from our hearts. It may be years before the bargain is understood, before the riddle is solved, before a story begins to take shape or make sense. The good stories must take it all in, all of it. In the in-between, there may only be questions and then a lying down. Sleeping with Jacob was a tenuous bargain. The fitful nights risked everything: the loss of the emotional strength that sustains the habit of laughter and play and that feeds the desire to know and piece together ever-growing fragments of new memories. But it was a story whose terms we thought we knew and accepted. Something of the nature of sacrifice had been part of our own rearing: as middle children of large families, as individuals whose religious faith centered on a giving up, on a tradition of stories that fostered an acceptance of the hard fact of death and the need to wait for the next day. This was the soft touch, the good that fed muscle and bone and imagination.

But we did not fully know.

If stories do not simply give a face to the good and the bad, the clever and the conniving, the pure and impure, but instead provide a framework within which to house meaning, to greet the unbidden guest, then the reader must remain vigilant. Guilt and blame can offer as much sanctuary as open hands and forgiveness. It is a hard truth that our stories shape how we come to know.

Sometimes we get lucky. The story that might have broken us has been lost or retold, and we can look back and learn. In the current narrative of autism, for instance, we do not attribute the cause of a child's withdrawal to parenting, to a failure to bond with or properly nurture a child. We know that it is a developmental disorder, a genetically wired way of knowing that shows itself most dramatically around the time that a child should be acquiring language and learning the cues that help establish familial and social ties. Not long ago, however, another narrative framed how doctors and parents saw autism. Oddly, the storyteller is a familiar figure, Bruno Bettelheim.

Less than a decade before penning *The Uses of Enchantment*, in 1967, Bettelheim published his influential study of autism entitled *The Empty Fortress: Infantile Autism and the Birth of the Self*. Having already gained a national and international reputation for research asserting that autism emerged from an individual's deep rejection of the world, he wrote of initially being disturbed by but curious about children whom he saw as deliberately turning their backs on the world. "If we could understand which isolated aspects of reality were so abortive of humanity as to snuff it out," he asserts in the introduction, "there might be something constructive we could do." Quite tragically, here is the story that he told: inadequate mothering at critical stages of development led to catastrophic rejection and resulted in various evils, including schizophrenia and autism. In other words, "refrigerator mothers," as they came to be called, inflicted psychological wounds severe enough to cause the child to reject the world and turn inward. In this narrative, little imaginative distance existed between the stepmother and witch of "Hansel and Gretel" and the flawed mothers of Bettelheim. Ultimately, parents were told that the child with autism could only be reborn in intensive therapy, separated from the mother, and outside the home. And so Bettelheim formed the Orthogenic School, a supposed sanctuary where the driven out, the Hansels and Gretels, were fed gingerbread and families waited for the return.

At one point, in fact, Bettelheim brings forward an illustrative reflection on the story of Hansel and Gretel. Drawing from an earlier psychological study, one that used the Grimms' tale to illuminate mother-child relationships, he directly connects the witch to the destructive mother of one of his schizophrenic patients. For this young girl in his clinic, it was discovered that she feared being baked and eaten by her mother. While he writes that the "nightmarish anxiety and her autism" evolved from her own imagination, he goes on to assign the cause of her condition to her mother's own difficulties with raising children. With this family, the father apparently had to choose between his daughter and his wife; he chose his wife.

What would it have meant to make such a choice? I can see the face of my wife across the kitchen table, weeping at the news of Jacob's diagnosis. I revisit the bins of Jacob's early years that Mary has tucked away in the basement: the medical records, teachers' notes, early drawings and finger paintings. In my recollecting, I catch her profile as she opens the door of our work room in the house on Lovell Street, asking when I will be done with my paper grading, her voice edged with anger. I sense her desperation and helplessness when the door shuts. And then my own anger. At times, I recall my relief at sleeping alone, of being released from the need to fight past my resentments or guilt to accept her embrace. If I let myself enter the rooms of those past years, I relive those evenings of uninterrupted silence, the long gaps in fragile conversations, and my own retreating inward.

But I have no memory that would undergird the embracing reach of Bettelheim's narrative: no cold maternity, no invitation to abandon a son or daughter. What I have is the memory of my son struggling to accommodate touch and sound, my holding his six-month-old body against my chest as I try to rock him to sleep. His head shifts to find the softness of my shoulder. I begin to whisper, then quietly sing: "Rockabye. Rockabye." With Sarah, the songs led to her heavy breathing, a rest so deep that I could take my right hand and lift sweaty strands of her hair to cool in the dark and press my nose against the back of her head to take in the scent of Baby Magic shampoo. But Jacob does not let me sing or take in his scent. He raises his head and lightly bumps my cheek, a signal, I soon understand, to stop these tender lyrics and end my noisy intimacies. It is an odd rejection, one to accept but puzzle over.

These seeming denials accumulated: an unwillingness to lie between Mary and me when he awoke early in the morning, a preference to have the blinds pulled down during the day, a loud, shrill crying when we played certain Barney the Dinosaur songs. We learned to pull away, to step back and watch, honoring his at-first endearing idiosyncrasies until the space grew, the language was lost, and the silence made us wonder and doubt. If we had not taken care of younger siblings, had not first raised Sarah and witnessed typical developmental thresholds, and had only Bettelheim's paradigm to understand Jacob's distance and withdrawal, we might have taken on the blame and lost ourselves in a devastating guilt.

Even now, though, I am drawn to the seductive logic of what I know is not true. After all, in the compelling case studies of *The Empty Fortress*, Bettelheim conveys absolute certainty that, with patience and love, the children's mysterious babbling and rituals could eventually be understood, that the gap could be bridged. In the face of such conviction, I confront my own lingering doubts. Did my own failings when responding to my son's early silence and shrieks, his pulling back from touch, form a kind of abandonment, the forsaking of his best attempts to communicate his own needs? Did I do enough to bridge that widening space between us? With such questions lingers the belief in the possibility of the next new intervention, the next breakthrough story that seems to say that autism is a condition to be erased or a "disease" to be cured, a temporary thing, not a different way of knowing and being.

Having lived, then, deep in the tempting realities of these hopes, I turned to Bettelheim's story of Joey, a rescued boy who believed that he was a machine when first arriving at the Orthogenic School. In this tale, Bettelheim interviews his former patient, asking why he had made his bed into a car. As I read this dialogue, I find myself wanting to be this all-knowing father figure. I want to believe that Jacob could be Joey, that he could one day bring home the redemptive treasure of his own inner world:

> **Joey.:** Well, I knew of course that a car is something that moves and it takes people places. After all, that's the whole reason it was invented; so people could go places faster. And also it was something in which a person was enclosed.
> **B.B.:** You liked this idea of being enclosed; it was important to you?
> **Joey.:** Yes.
> **B.B.:** Why? What were you afraid would happen if you weren't enclosed?
> **Joey.:** Well, I think the main reason behind my wanting to be enclosed was I think when I started coming closer to people, I very often. . . I'd have fantasies about a car or anything that moved on wheels that was enclosed and I'd have a fantasy that I was in it myself. Well, I'd always picture that somebody else was in it with me.
> **B.B.:** So it wasn't just to protect yourself against others?
> **Joey.:** No...
> **B.B.:** It was also to have somebody with you all the time? Who wouldn't leave you?
> **Joey.:** Yes. You know, it was just a few months after I first came here that I started to have such a fantasy. I know I never had a fantasy like that before, except on very rare occasions.

In this striking dialogue, it all seems to come down to self-protection, to the desire to reach out without the fear of abandonment. In listening to this drama, a script that Bettelheim would never purge of the mother's and father's role in causing autism, I can feel the tug of guilt. For parents, Joey's story gestures toward the fantasy that ever haunts the imagination: the revelatory conversation that explains the past and invites forgiveness, the cure that comes from the profound sacrifice of unconditional love.

How can we discern what stories will bring us home? How can we protect ourselves from looking back with regret or succumbing to guilt? How can we frame the story without turning our backs upon the harsh realities that must be seen and told? Ironically, in *The Empty Fortress*, Bruno Bettelheim offers a compelling acknowledgment of this dilemma, this struggle to come to some true story in the face of private evils, this desire to confront inner demons yet go beyond the self to a fuller empathy with others. Underscoring the need to sacrifice much to enter the "child's private world," he confesses that "[t]his will always, to some degree, mean a descent to one's own hell, however far behind one has left it," that it will "become a self-confrontation as one offers oneself to the other." In my reading of the legacy of *The Empty Fortress*, however, I learned that Bettelheim misrepresented his own credentials as a psychologist and, at times, the research that fostered his reputation. That he demanded that the world change their reading of autism, that people see the possibility of connection through intensive treatment, offers little solace. To the many families devoured by the story of their own "supposed" abandonment, to the mothers unable to retrieve years of fighting an evil that never was and to the fathers seduced by the bitter absolution, his care for the children seems like a witch's promise, a sweetness that forebodes fire and ash.

I have another story to tell. Because it is true, it includes the potential for good and evil. When I tell it, I must then listen to the desire that it narrates; I must watch for the unnamed yearning. Here is the only absolute: no matter what, I cannot leave the forest.

Here is my version of the old Grimms' folktale. The stepmother did not abandon the children and die. One day, when the woodcutter left early, she took them to a clearing near the edge of the forest. She told them stories of magic stones that caught the moonlight, of bread crumbs that drifted along the hardened edges of forest paths, and of gingerbread houses deep in the woods. At mid-day, she took out the last of the bread and handed the small crusts to Hansel and Gretel. Whether it was the heat or the weariness from their hunger or the cadence of the father's distant chopping, they slipped into a deep sleep. When the mother awoke, the children were gone. In her grief, she ran into the forest and soon lost herself. When the father returned home and found that his wife and children were not there, he called until his throat dripped blood. In his sorrow, his limbs succumbed to a dark magic, the same that overtook his wife, and he fell into a stupor. In the days and weeks that followed, he spent the waking hours clearing a path in the trees until his fingers grew stiff and callused. Villagers still claim they can hear the mother's weeping and the father's axe echoing in the forest.

Even with this story, it is possible to blame the mother, to overlook her storytelling and bread-giving and emphasize a lack of diligence. Should she not have anticipated the early waking, the children's desire to find the gingerbread house? It is possible to reproach the father, to see the work as another sign of abandonment. Should he not have remained with his family at such a moment, at a time of such risk? But, with different sympathies and imaginings, we might discern instead the evils of fate, the dark days that come by accident or from human frailty, from the sleep that cannot be avoided, the sleep that is the sign itself of the most vigilant waking. We could attune our senses to the things left unwritten: the deep silence of the mother's despondent tread and the imprint of pine needles upon the knees, the delay between the contact and sound of the axe, like the catch in the throat before the release of grief. Eventually, however, we might get lost in all the possible meanings, wandering between bitterness and compassion, holding forth the possibilities like torchlight in the dark pitch, seeing that, in the end, the blackness flickers as enchantingly as the light. In these times and places, what will save us? What will bring us out?

Weeks before his tenth birthday, my wife and I began a nighttime chant. "Jacob," we took turns saying, "After your birthday, you will sleep alone." "All big kids sleep alone," we lied. At first, we sensed a fear or concern. "Not by my own," he initially voiced, "Not by my own." But something in his demeanor also conveyed an acceptance, a readiness to embrace this change. And then, on his birthday, something magical happened: he settled into bed, covered his head with the sheet and blanket, and said good night.

Many partners do not get this far in the story. The leaving is not possible; the sleeping is the last potential magic. Too much grief resides in the hardest of facts: a son whose future has no shared bed and longing, whose silent vigil is a sleeping alone unto death. Even if the storytellers have gotten this far, they may have yet to know the full terms of the bargain, how words can both free and imprison with their own plot line and logic, how no one memory provides the key. They may have yet to learn that they are not writing to an ending or moral but a taste of blood in the throat.

How much more should I tell? I can imagine how Mary and I closed the door for what must have seemed like the first time. I can feel how much our bodies must have ached to be touched, to be known again, how much we wanted to begin anew. But I can also hear the questions that can only come by wandering alone so far and so deep. Did you not hear me calling? Could you not let go of the axe handle and venture deeper into the forest? I wonder if we can accept this coming home, the seeming accident of it. I wonder how far we can go now that the crumbs have blown away, how much ground we must cover to get beyond blame and anger to the scent of bread and pine.

We have all, no doubt, heard of Pandora's box, the one that contained the evil and misery of the world. In one version of the story, hope alone remained inside, the lid being shut before she could escape. I am still puzzling over what this means. Is it that the world has no place for hope, that hope cannot long co-exist in the presence of sickness or sleeplessness? Is it that hope is still contained in a jar, awaiting release, that it is like a precious thing held back or held inside?

On some nights when I lay awake and hear the cadence of Mary's breathing, I let myself tell stories. I imagine that I am the mythmaker, heartsick with the legacy of war or famine or love lost, or, more simply, thinking of a son sleeping fitfully in the dark. For a moment, I dream that once upon a time—in some distant era and place—I sat pondering the Pandora myth, wondered aloud about Hope, began to retell the old story, only this time with the need to account for the origins of all things, good and bad, the moment before the lid snapped shut. Then, just before my own breathing grows deeper, I imagine a distant voice and reach for some sign to cast forth. "You, listener with the story in your hands," it says. "Remember that with the proper telling, hope, too, can be unleashed. But here is the hardest of bargains: once you enter the story, you cannot leave. Always remember, you cannot leave."

II. Sites

CROYDEN AVENUE SCHOOL

FLOOD PLAIN

THE WILD DAYS

CROYDEN AVENUE SCHOOL

Backing into a small hill not far north of West Main Street, just east of Drake Road, Croyden Avenue School formerly served children and teens with physical and cognitive disabilities. To the west of the building lies a fenced-in playground cut here and there by the scars of old sandboxes or the haphazard paths of children's play. One or two streaks of sand lead nowhere, or perhaps simply the somewhere of a jungle gym or seesaw long cut from cement anchors. The grass never quite fills in these absences, and, with the thin powdering of the first snow, the hieroglyphic smudges of past recesses show through the whiteness.

Nothing is ever canceled out. Nothing ever remains the same.

FLOOD PLAIN

With my four-year-old son, Jacob, I enter the front doors of Croyden Avenue School and move toward the steps that descend to the classroom for children with autism. He lingers at the top of the stairs and, as most days, pauses at his reflection in the glass walls. The ritual is not new so I wait, calling his name once or twice out of habit, before directing him down the steps to his room.

After returning to my car, feeling as if I have set Jacob adrift within the hurried current of the morning, I sometimes enter my own sensory memories of grade school: the sound of stiff new jeans scissoring down corridors, the sharp cries across a playground, the art room odor of crayon, the touch of white paste and papier-mâché, the brilliant reds and purples of thick-textured paintings dried and cracking like late summer creek beds.

I remember walking down to the playground of my Northwest Iowa elementary school, Arctic Cat snowmobile boots tossing fragments of snow from my heels, blackened mittens on my hands, a basketball tucked under my right arm. Alone, I launched shot after shot at a hoop positioned on the end of the asphalt surface in front of the school. Before long, the ball grew slick and harder to balance on the wide mittens. But, in my imagination, I was always a point behind and poised for the miraculous last shot, for some sign that divinity still intervened for those who held out in the cold. When it was well below freezing, I wore a ski mask. On those frigid dusks of mid-winter, the moisture from my breath would dampen the thin material, and the cotton would freeze and harden. If the cloth rubbed awkwardly against my cheeks, I would take it off and give life back to the frozen mask by blowing my hot breath through the thin icy layers. When it grew dark not long after five, I would slowly walk over to the west side of the building, position my forearms on the brick ledge of the window casement, kick my feet against the wall, and balance precariously to see the time on the classroom clock above the cursive alphabet.

I find it odd to have such intimate awareness of this past self, this child who I was that shares no knowledge of who I have become, who comes unexpected and stays only so long as I pause to follow the memory. I watch as he pushes himself back from the wall of the school, bends to embrace the ball, and tightly shuts his eyes to melt the ice that has laced together his long lashes. Hurrying home across the small, snow-covered baseball field, he slides upon a patch of ice and playfully kicks a small drift of snow. Around him, the wind has risen slightly, and the streetlight catches the crystals of scattering snowflakes before they disappear into the shadows. I follow their scattering into the dark before turning the key and driving out of the Croyden parking lot.

Later that morning, I wait on a bench outside the front office. Jacob climbs the stairs; his hand glides up the rail. He wears his backpack unlike other children who know how other children wear their backpacks. He backs into my embrace. As I kneel before him, I gently turn his shoulders until his face is before mine, until I can feel the faint touch of his breath against my lips. "Jacob, what do you say?" He does not raise his chin. "Look at Daddy, Jacob." He lifts his head, but our eyes are like repelling magnets. I raise my hand and hold his chin. He is still learning to see me, to acknowledge my gaze. When he finally fixes his eyes momentarily on mine, it is hard to know whether he apprehends me in a way that I understand. It is a daydreamer's glance, a glimpse of some reverie initiated by my voice. I seem to exist as a memory, not flesh and blood.

"Hi, Daddy." His voice is nourishment, a food that fills me.

Driving home, I ask him if he had a good day. He disregards my question and begins the motif that will become the ritualistic chant of the afternoon.

"Watch TV."

"First lunch and then TV."

"Watch TV. Oh, yeah, watch TV." The "Oh, yeah" is from TV.

"First we eat lunch, then TV," I reply calmly.

"Haveta gonna draw! Haveta gonna draw!"

"Would you like to draw when we get home, Jacob?"

"Haveta gonna draw!"

"When we get home."

When we get home, I draw. I start to sketch in pencil the small Mickey Mouse logo from his *Beauty and the Beast* video box. He watches the ritual acutely; it is always new. He is wary lest I should color the yellow shoes red or the blue hat black. Erase it, he gestures, when I begin the third Mickey. I have learned to draw gently so that my erasing will not leave marks.

"This one," Jacob says, pointing to the *Walt Disney Productions* lettering. I loop the large "W" and "D" with practiced flourish as my son chants one of the Disney musical motifs. Then he sees something wrong, something that I do not notice. It has to do with the "t" in "Walt."

"This one."

I hear urgency in his voice. I look closely at the letter. I amend.

"This one," he insists. He traces the letter on the table as if I can see on the plastic tablecloth the vivid design in his mind. I watch his fingers; in my palm, his hand would disappear, it seems so small.

"Show me," I say, handing him the pencil. On most days, he refuses. Today, he takes it. He presses hard on the lead and the cross in the "t" slides toward the "D" like a train wreck.

"Oh no, look what you dee-id!" Jacob laments, mixing pronouns and using a phrase and intonation gathered from a Curious George video. Or is it I who he sees as the curious little monkey, creating a mess of things again?

I pick up the pencil and try again and again. Finally, among the scattered drawings that litter the table, I succumb to the frustration, to the persistent demand of these rigid patterns. I toss the pencil down and say "this one" is my "t," that it is the way I will draw the "t," and that Jacob should draw his own "t."

"Draw it!" he replies.

"No, you do it!"

"Daddy do it!"

"No, Jacob do it!"

Suddenly, the papers take to the air, and Jacob runs screaming into the living room. More colors than I can name spread through the room: red and blue and green Duplos clack against the sides of the couch and picture window, the yellow of the box glances off my arm, and the glare of sunlight catches them all, a prism undone. His words break against me, "Want to try again! Want to try again!" In these moments, Jacob will suddenly look directly at me and find the pronouns and names that have fallen off the edges of his sentences. "I want to try again, please Daddy." And I wonder what memory held the syntax of this pleading.

At the end of the week, I again arrive shortly after mid-day to pick up Jacob from Croyden. I sit upon the bench along a wall in the front lobby and lean back against the red brick. Children are arriving for the afternoon. I hear the whir of the elevator of the first bus. From its side emerges a young girl in a wheel chair. Her head tilts against the head cushion. Her smile unsettles me. She is glancing somewhere I am not, but I sit up, eager to greet her at the door. I am learning to look into her eyes.

Outside a few flakes of snow begin to suggest themselves, lingering like the descending ash of the burnings of late fall. As I try to make out the snow from the gray sky, another memory urges itself forward. I am twelve and on my stingray bicycle pedaling through an empty street to a 6:30 a.m. basketball practice. It is mid December. A night snow has covered the street with a blanket of white; except for the shadows cast by the intervals of streetlights and the predictable angles of houses and sidewalks, the landscape has few boundaries. For a moment, I close my eyes and ride blind, until, feeling the thrill of pedaling just beyond some imaginary limit, I stop to look over my shoulder. Behind me, the wandering indentations of my tires, like the frozen paths of small streams, fill with snow; the more distant banks are diminished to thin creases of shadow. The street stretches forth like a flood plain fertile with the meanderings of past river channels. It is a world that I had not seen, and so I let myself linger in the space between past and present, this borderless landscape of beauty and loss.

More buses and cars move up to the curb. A few parents enter with their sons or daughters. One child catches my eye; he seems older than the others. After the boy leaves to go down the stairs to his classroom, his mother takes a seat on the other end of my bench. When our eyes meet, I introduce myself and am about to tell her about Jacob just as she is called into the office to talk with the school psychologist. She hesitates a moment, and I sense that she does not want to do the unkindness of not hearing my story. But I glance toward the office to divert her eyes and assure her. "Perhaps another time," I say.

After she goes, I can feel the vibrations of my son's unuttered name on my tongue and the way my lungs had filled to hold the beginnings of an unformed tale. For a moment, I see myself through her eyes—an eager father whose son now plays in a place previously unimagined and who pauses on the threshold between a world just opening up and another seemingly canceled out. I glimpse the distinct outlines of that person that Jacob has begun to erase. At first, he remains distant, but I coax the ghost forward with my yearning. Wordlessly, he lifts his head as if in a daydream and meets my gaze. It is not my son's face; it is mine. This lost and wandering self wishes to speak; it cannot, and I find myself gently leaning forward. If I can hold his glance for just a moment, I wonder, perhaps that is enough. And then I think back to the woman's eyes and the healing pause of a hesitant recognition, a shared longing, a hunger for the retelling or a new telling of a story she well knew. It is what we both needed, this amending, this wash of words.

Jacob has had a rough morning, his aide says. He had to have some quiet time because he would not join snack group. During recess, he stood at the top of the Purple Mountain, a favorite climbing toy, and danced on one leg. Even now Jacob is dancing and laughing and saying "Lucky get down! Lucky get down!" Around me I can feel the movement of other children exiting and entering through the sliding glass door.

We walk outside and before I can stop him he races to the slide at the side of the building, the wind blowing back the hood of his fall jacket. I run after him. He refuses to come with me until I bribe him with the promise of french fries at McDonald's. It takes fifteen more minutes to get to the car. My ears are numb from the cold air; my palms still feel the steel handles of the slide.

Once home, we draw. I search for unmarked paper in the piles of half-done drawings atop the refrigerator and kitchen counter. We have run through the ream of blank paper, so I gather four pieces that promise the easiest erasing and carefully remove half-written words and the limbs of cartoon characters.

"Haveta gonna draw *Walt Disney Productions*," Jacob commands.

I take up the pencil, bracing myself for the fight I see coming. When I get to the "t," Jacob moves off his chair and, clutching the video box, crowds in upon my lap.

"This one. This one." His voice is calm, and I am surprised by how the words seem empty of memory, how the phrases merge together quiet, encouraging, and full of trust.

As I am about to retrace the lines from our previous play, I see something that I had not seen before. Just above the small curve of his pointing finger, barely showing through the dark background behind the lettering, a small loop appears where I thought I had seen a straight cross line. It was never a straight line. It was always a small but clearly discernible loop. With this revelation, I see the smaller letters of the words anew: the way the crossing middle of the "a" touches, but barely touches the initial "W" in "Walt," the way the "s" in "Disney" keeps curling, how the final "y" reflects the hurry of the last letter of any signature. I let the pencil rest for a moment and smell the back of my son's head. I press my lips against his cheek until he lifts his shoulder, leans away, and says, "Haveta gonna draw the 't.'"

Slowly, gently, I press the lead to the page. After I finish, Jacob holds the paper in his hand and, satisfied, lets it fall. It slices the air and then rises for just a moment, suspended, as if hesitating playfully before a final slide to the floor.

When I was young, I would frequently stare out the north window of my house. Beyond the railroad tracks just twenty feet from our garage and not far from the highway running parallel to the tracks spread the flat expanse of a field. I was five and struck with awe at that endless stretch of furrows stitched so seamlessly to the distant horizon, and I stumbled into the question of beginnings. What started all this? What came before the feel of the field upon my eyes, before the dirt itself, before the pulling back of ice and snow? At times, it seems as if I began living that day. The spirit demands the expansiveness of such imaginings.

We walk on vast flood plains. Beneath our feet, the firmness of the ground seems to confirm the permanence of the river channel. To hold up the banks, we press rocks and concrete, believing that our labors can prevent the slide of soil. But there is no telling what may happen when the snow thaws or the next rain comes. The bend in the distance may straighten and, suddenly, the landscape is no longer recognizable. We learn in time that we do not control the ultimate shape of things.

Living with Jacob is about more than allowing the language of his mind to erase the chalk lines of my own patterns. It is about unexpected intersections, the willingness to walk blind, to discern shadows in the lay of the land. It is about the painful unburdening that comes when the mind expands to see anew.

THE WILD DAYS

"Jacob, take the block *out* of the cup."

"Jacob, take the block *out* of the cup."

In front of me and my fifteen students, the screen lights up with the video of my three-year-old son crowded onto a small chair. It is the second week of our freshman writing seminar entitled Crossing Borders: Autism and Other Ways of Knowing. We are watching a scene from Jacob's first year at Croyden Avenue School.

Everything conspires to set severe limitations: the back of Jacob's chair pinches a cubicle wall, a small table to the right rubs against his arm, a wall frames the left edge of the screen. The teacher sits just to the left, facing my son, a small block in one hand and a plastic cup in the other. When making the request, she amplifies her gestures. Her left hand rises in the air when she says, "Jacob"; it traces an exaggerated arc toward the cup at the command. It is hard to know whether my son sees the demonstration. His eyes follow some inner drama; his feet jab at his teacher's knees.

"Jacob, take the block out of the cup."

The movement between child and teacher is a rough dance. Forcefully, without anger or impatience, she lifts my son repeatedly back onto the chair, slides her own chair back as Jacob tries to kick her, and puts the table in its proper place after he has squeezed between it and the back wall. When he finally takes the wooden block from the cup, she tickles him, the form of reinforcement that has replaced M & Ms. Halfway through the ten-minute segment, Jacob rebels, grabs at the teacher with his pinching hands, and eventually succumbs to inconsolable weeping. He holds one note of his wailing, an operatic grieving that empties his lungs.

When I close my eyes, I endure the sudden play of another memory on my own inner screen: Mary and I behind a one-way mirror, an hour of observing Jacob crying, hitting, and scratching a behavioral psychologist. She pins his legs between her knees and refuses to let him go. "Look at me," she states repeatedly. "Look at me." She wants him to look at her face, to attend with eye contact to her presence in the room; he will not. We watch, quarantined inside the adjoining room, wondering if any amount of viewing will inoculate us from this condition of too much feeling.

Eventually, I survey my students watching my son and his teacher. I play the video to provide a glimpse of one intervention model for those newly diagnosed with autism, discrete trial training or Applied Behavioral Analysis. In doing so, I hope to illustrate the kinds of scenes that they will see in their visit to Croyden, moments that flash again and again in the minds of parents and children. Looking over the class, I observe how a few students stare with a clinical curiosity. I study how others begin to turn their heads so that they will only see the screen at an angle, how some move their arms to their chest, how they work to beat back the uneven breathing that comes with heartache, how they too try to hold the emotion of new things in the heart and lungs.

In the moments when I am standing before my class or poised to tell a story of Jacob or myself aloud or in writing, I feel this haunting dividedness. I am the father in or alongside the pictures, the one holding up my son for the viewer, acting the immediate and intimate role of a loving parent. Yet, I am also the camera holder, the chronicler, the editor, the anthropologist, the seemingly dispassionate onlooker reeling in and analyzing the bits and pieces for meaning, seeking the story that will hold everything together, striving to formulate a language to bridge the gaps. At times, as in the moment behind the one-way mirror, I am simultaneously the father and observer, the fraught figure with numbing memories and clinical knowledge, watching without power to change what I see or with theories that force me to hold back and let the experiment play out for the good of the patient. It is wrong to call this type of witnessing cold or unfeeling; rather, it is the kind that fills one's chest to bursting. The only way to keep the body whole is to hear or read of another observer's history behind the glass.

I remember my son's hands, the fists shuddering at the initial wailing. In his first weeks, I placed the end of my smallest finger upon his left palm and turned it gently until his hand clutched. Within a month, he learned to balance a small bottle upon the fat beneath his thumbs. When he tired of the bottle's weight, I tucked my thumb and little finger into the cocoons of his hands and held it for him; I felt the sticky sweat and smelled the sweet milky odor rising from his smooth skin. Before words, his hands negotiated the intimate spaces of the world.

With only a limited ability to use language as he approached his second birthday, Jacob utilized his small hands to voice his wants and frustrations. After positioning me in front of the television, he would gently press the back of his hand into my palm and guide my fingers toward the cable box. When I came to know the meaning of this beckoning, whether used to encourage turning on a favorite show or to get a book from the shelf, I found that I had begun to acquire a unique vocabulary, a language that depended on knowing the material things that fell within his reach and mine. An onlooker might first be unable to discern how an uplifting of the back of the hand into my palm or the more urgent gripping of my fingers and then tossing of my arm communicated different emotions and desires. How could another person understand that a well-known book could be found without the use of words, that the empty space around our bodies and the bookshelf could come alive with meaningful signs and gestures?

In those years, he seemed like a wild child at times and, as Mary and I came to quickly understand, required constant supervision. We began to feel imprisoned by Jacob's seeming inattention to the world or his obsessive attention to sometimes inexplicable wants. Such a reality became most evident when we would have friends over or co-host college events near our house on the edge of campus.

During these times, we would alternately assign ourselves to Jacob, diligently monitoring his movements and intervening when he acted inappropriately. He would wander between clusters of faculty members when he came outdoors while Mary or I, rather self-consciously, followed him as if we were tethered to his wrist. For most people, he was just an active little boy; for others, I feared, he represented a hyperactive child who needed discipline or whose parents were a bit overprotective. While the sights and sounds of such gatherings must have been overwhelming for Jacob, he seemed to enjoy what appeared to be the communal nature of food and drink, gulping from unattended cups of lemonade and grabbing finger food from abandoned plates. He foraged among the tables as if an untamed boy unaware of the civil rules of human gatherings.

On other occasions, Jacob held his ground on some desire and would not be moved—or could not be stopped in his need to get beyond our imposed boundaries. As we became more knowledgeable about the nature of autism, we came to recognize that he had difficulty transitioning between various activities and places. To go from outdoors back into our house, then, often prompted his repeated attempts to escape down the sidewalk that led to Stetson Chapel, his favorite retreat at the center of campus. He would face our front door, his back to his desired destination, and, after a couple minutes of slowly shuffling his heels down the sidewalk, reach a point beyond the more urgent edge of our calling, turn and run. To bring him home, we would have to sprint after Jacob and carry him back kicking and screaming through a gauntlet of more or less sympathetic stares.

In the winter prior to his third birthday, Mary and I had Jacob assessed by a speech therapist, a social worker, a psychologist, and an occupational therapist at Croyden. I remember watching him go through the physical tests and table play with a sense of pride. As Mary joined the psychologist behind the one-way mirror in an adjoining room, I sat just off his shoulder, encouraging him, following him from toy to toy. I had to fight the urge to offer a running narrative of my son's seemingly special behaviors: "Jacob likes to arrange magnetic letters like movie credits…. He has great balance…. He lines toys up for hours." After the formal testing, as we all got ready to leave, Jacob noticed a mirror standing against the wall. He was fascinated with his image in it. He danced and walked back and forth in front of the tall length of glass. The act seemed so child-like that I enjoyed the play of it until I noticed the two observers exchange glances.

Two weeks later, the psychologist on the assessment team met with us at our home. She indicated that Jacob had been diagnosed as autistic. Calmly and gently, she reviewed the report, underscoring why his behaviors indicated autism. She especially noted the language deficits—and the tendency to lose words. She recommended some readings, suggesting that when we were ready we could review materials that discuss the long-term possibilities. She said that autism was not curable; it was a life-long condition. She noted that, because Jacob appeared to be so high-functioning, he might especially benefit from early and intensive educational interventions to build vocabulary and learn social skills. When she left, Mary and I sat at the table, glancing at the materials before us. We did not want to say goodbye to the Jacob we had imagined forward in time, the brother who would accompany his sister to the same schools, who would converse with her about teachers they might have shared. In our mind's eye, we caught glimpses of this unimagined child when he grew into awkward manhood and then we wept for him and for ourselves. We had no story for this moment and this place.

I do not now know what came first: my father-minded browsing that led to Mordicai Gerstein's *The Wild Boy*, or my teacher-driven research on autism in Uta Frith's *Autism: Explaining the Enigma*. They merge together in my consciousness, this story of the child Victor and his father-doctor Jean Marc Gaspard Itard. I do know that, along with the many parents I befriended in Kalamazoo, Itard became a vital partner. In putting into writing his own vivid recollections, he not only deepened the historical layers of autism; he helped me understand the nature of my dividedness.

I first saw Gerstein's beautifully-illustrated tale in a Cambridge, Massachusetts bookstore during a research trip. For ten days, I had been trekking from library to library in Washington, D.C., Bethesda, Maryland, and the Cambridge-Boston area, investigating eighteenth and nineteenth-century notions of the mind and higher states of consciousness. The research centered on Edgar Allan Poe and Margaret Fuller, antebellum writers who had been influenced by early understandings of hypnotic states and the impact of words and nonverbal gestures upon readers. In my last days of the research trip, I began to use my breaks from dusty volumes and microfilm to look for gifts in the area bookstores.

While browsing, I saw *The Wild Boy*, a book that was based upon the remarkable story of the young boy of Aveyron, later named Victor, who was taken from the forest of southern France in 1799. The book jacket captures the boy in a graceful leap with yellow, brown, orange, and purple leaves blowing from his hands. Below his feet, the tall grass seems to genuflect to his body; above his dark, flowing but tangled hair, a white cloud frames the blue sky and fringes the mountains on the left margin. "Once there was a boy who lived in the mountain forests of southern France," the book opens. "He lived completely alone, without mother, father, or friends. . . . He knew how to live in the wild woods. He knew which plants, berries, and roots would nourish him. He was always hungry." As I turned the pages, I recalled how, in Frith's book, she had asserted that Victor was one of the first documented accounts of an individual on the spectrum, though, in that period, doctors initially considered him to be a deaf-mute whose isolation caused his uncivilized and unsocial behaviors. In fact, for the time, physicians and philosophers saw Victor as a kind of savage, a person akin to peoples being discovered in the wilderness places of the new world.

Flipping through the storybook that evening, I grew increasingly fascinated with Victor as well as the figure of Itard, the character Gerstein first draws observing the unnamed boy, shoeless, huddled in a corner at the Institute for Deaf-Mutes and then watching him scatter dry leaves on a pond. On another page, he depicts Itard introducing Victor to a game with cups: "The doctor had an idea: he showed Victor a walnut, then put it under a cup and mixed it up among other cups." Then, after hours and hours marked by the labor of endless instruction, of striving to teach concepts and language, Itard joins Victor before bed in the blue, candle-lit darkness. Amid the full moon light, the doctor-father looks on with questions: "I wonder what he sees, thought the doctor. I wonder what he feels. I wonder…." With these last lines, I felt the bond of a common experience; across more than two centuries, Itard and I sat together, hands and arms trying to find a way to embrace and teach, hold and hold at a distance, for some end that we could not yet fully envision.

Knowing some lesson resided in these similar memories, I returned to the representation of Victor that Itard documented in his book *The Wild Boy of Aveyron*. In doing so, I discovered my son in this distant child. In Victor's effort to communicate, for instance, I see a similar dependence upon the hands to express desires. When narrating his effort to teach the boy "the use of speech," Itard describes the especially difficult process of language development, noting how "our young savage" does not use words but other "expressive signs" that capture subtle differences in meaning. In other words, the young boy uses physical signs, not words, gestures that, like verbal language, convey a range of wants. He reveals how Victor would retrieve objects necessary for his walk as a signal for the daily excursion and how he would show his wish for milk by "presenting a wooden porringer which, on going out, he never forgets to put in his pocket…." In an especially poignant section, the book details the boy's effort to communicate his wish to be pushed in a wheelbarrow: "…as soon as the inclination arises, if nobody comes to satisfy it, he returns to the house, takes someone by the arm, leads him to the garden and puts in his hands the handles of the wheelbarrow, into which he then climbs. If his first invitation is resisted he leaves his seat, turns to the handles of the wheelbarrow, rolls it for some turns, and places himself in it again; imagining doubtless, that if his desires are not fulfilled after all this, it is not because they are not clearly expressed." Later, Itard refers to this mode of communication as a "pantomime language," a language that he notes can be used by others to present wants as well. He observes how the governess, Madame Guerin, expresses her wish to have Victor get some water by simply showing him the pitcher and turning it upside down. Reading about these gestures, I felt the touch of my own son's fingers in the muscle memory of being guided to a book shelf or pulled to a wagon handle. To read of such moments is to return differently to the language of my own past and to accept, even now, the gentle hand clasp of my teenage son. I can receive the gesture as part of his idiom, his desire to communicate and connect over the years, not as a past memory of what was absent or lost.

When embracing these joint experiences, I also confront moments that I would like to erase from the record, mistakes arising from the frustration that can come with developing a father-teacher relationship with boys like Victor and Jacob. Having borne Victor's tendency to launch into "inopportune gaiety" or to drift toward inattention when asked to distinguish distinct sounds, Itard resorts to negative reinforcement, striking the boy's fingers lightly and then more vigorously with a drum stick. Behind blindfolds, Victor first treats the blows "as a joke and in his glee became even livelier." With a last harsher rap, however, the child understands:

> I saw in the lad's clouded expression how the pain of the blow was lost in the feeling of insult. Tears rolled down from under his bandage. I hastened to raise it but whether from perplexity or fear or from a profound occupation of the inner senses, he persisted in keeping his eyes closed although freed of the bandage. I cannot describe how unhappy he looked with his eyes thus closed and with tears escaping from them every now and then. Oh! how ready I was on this occasion, as on many others, to give up my self-imposed task and regard as wasted the time that I had already given to it! How many times did I regret ever having known this child, and freely condemn the sterile and inhuman curiosity of the men who first tore him from his innocent and happy life!

Of all Itard's extensive reporting on the "wild boy," this lamenting haunts me. I know the old days when I had taken Jacob forcibly from the computer chair, ripped a favorite drawing, and thrown a Walkman on the floor. Against his iron will and fixations, I have yelled and slammed doors. And, if I have never voiced the desire to be free of my son, I have retreated into a depression and despair that functioned as a kind of abandonment. I know Victor's tears, then, and my own need for exclamations to mark this crushing doubt and regret. In those moments when I replay the Croyden days or the afternoons of shouting in frustration, I hear Itard's one-syllable utterance rise in my throat. "Oh!" Could I have provided more time for transitioning and discerned more finely when the gesture called out for connection, not isolation? Could I have given into the invitation to laugh, set the task aside, and become a father again? All of these memories! All these wild interiors, my own feral days, moving across the mind!

If I need Itard's memories to confront the past and utter my own confessions, I also require them to work against a guilt-induced narrowness of vision, an unforgiving impulse that leads me to forget tender acts because they have left no scars or material artifacts of some past problem solving. Focusing too hard and long on things endured, after all, is a kind of editing that can hide the finer strands and textures required of the fullest remembering.

Something from the end of Mordicai Gerstein's *The Wild Boy*, the illustration of Itard's hand upon Victor's head, led me to one such remembrance in *The Wild Boy of Aveyron* and to the potential for a healing expansiveness. Confessing that his charge holds more affection for Madame Guerin than himself, the doctor nonetheless concludes one of his sections with this gentle recollection: "…when I go to the house in the evening just after he has gone to bed, his first movement is to sit up for me to embrace him, then to draw me to him by seizing my arm and making me sit upon his bed, after which he usually takes my hand, carries it to his eyes, his forehead, the back of his head, and holds it with his upon these parts for a very long time." Until I read of this nighttime scene, I did not realize how much I had forgotten about Jacob, how so much of our intimate heritage had been lost. When I used to put him to bed, he would cover his face with my hand. Eventually, it evolved into a game. I would put my hand above his head as it lay upon the pillow. I would bring my fingers and thumb together, count without words to three by letting my thumb rise, then my "pointer" finger, then the middle one. After a quick suspension of this fan of fingers, I would utter, "Gah," and bring my hand down gently upon his face, wriggling it as he giggled and giggled. For years, this odd ritual was a part of our bedtime routine.

There is one more partner in this co-remembering: French filmmaker Francois Truffaut. He brings forth one last thing to watch, another play of images upon the screen, one more way to be witness to the past without succumbing to it. In the spring of 1964, Truffaut discovered the story of Itard and Victor after reading a review of Lucien Malson's 1964 book *Les Enfants sauvages: Mythe et realite* (*Wild Children: Myth and Reality*). In the volume, he would have come across the call for opening oneself up to other experiences. "Man's is not a closed life," Malson writes, arguing that an openness guides our encounters, that before contact with others our lives are "thin and insubstantial as mist," and that we require a "milieu—the presence of others." According to one biography of the director, Truffaut went out and bought ten copies of *Wild Children*, as he often did when he found a source for possible films. Malson's book, which includes Itard's writings, obviously spoke to Truffaut's own history of an unhappy childhood, timely mentoring, and, as a result, an enduring advocacy for abused and neglected youth. Almost immediately, Truffaut assigned Jean Gruault to develop a script, which the filmmaker ultimately helped co-write, that became one of his most respected films, *The Wild Child*.

The documentary-like accuracy of the film also betrays a hidden but telling history. Truffaut could guide the visual enactment of Victor's emergence because he had seen children with autism; his imagination and sympathies had been shaped through the presence of others on the spectrum. While overseeing the writing of the script, he had helped produce a film on the disorder: Fernand Deligny's and Jean-Pierre Daniel's *Le Moindre Geste* (*The Least Gesture* 1965). In their biography *Truffaut*, Antoine de Baecque and Serge Toubiana write that, one year before shooting *The Wild Child*, the director asked an assistant to go observe a boy "whose behavior, according to Deligny, was surprisingly similar to Victor's." In November of 1968,

Truffaut wrote Deligny concerning the boy: "Your description of his behavior is so similar to what Itard described in his writings and to what we want to achieve in the film that I find it extremely disconcerting.... In any case, I think your boy should serve as our model in selecting the boy who will actually play the part and should inspire us for his style of bodily comportment." Though *The Wild Child* does not push the view that Victor had autism or even suggest that Truffaut understood this possibility, it is driven by the desire to render the abandoned child with the same painstaking care as Itard.

And there is one other unique feature of *The Wild Child* that arises in the various reviews and interviews, one that speaks to the human need to negotiate the desire to be part of and yet observe and shape from a distance: for the first time in any of his films, Truffaut chose to be both actor and director. While no one reason may have led Truffaut to step from behind the camera and enter the screen as Itard, it is possible to see this choice as reflecting a deeper desire, the wish to experience the past even more fully, to release himself into Itard's and Victor's story. When he first read of the doctor/teacher and his charge, Truffaut must have felt the transformative influence of those hands upon the face, the child's physical rebellion, the miraculous effect of a pantomime language. Is this not the longing of any reader or viewer, to accept the healing trauma of a shared intimacy—and to hold its potential inside like a memory that protects in the purging reach of its joy and sorrow?

At night, when the repetitions of Jacob's world overwhelm me, I leave the house and walk the streets of my neighborhood. Where we live, the road serves as a broad walkway; the dead-end street and infrequent traffic make for a safe passage beneath the canopy of trees. I try to listen to the way the breeze sounds when it spools through the limbs and leaves, the way the cottonwood translates wind into the sound of small waves curling along a rocky lake shore. I want movement and space, the touch of wind on my face. On these nights, I find myself re-playing events that led me outside: the frustration at my son's persistent request to buy an item on eBay, his urgent hands holding a printed page with the image and cost of some video or his hundredth drawing of Prince Charming kissing Cinderella. I cut and paste as I walk, letting the memories flicker against the dark like a neighbor's television flashing through picture windows.

I am remembering and imagining now, projecting one thing and then another and another. I am thinking of Victor when the rain calls him outside to sit and sway at the edge of a pond. I am hearing Itard's voice; it is mine, reading aloud. "I have often stopped for hours with inexpressible delight to consider him in this situation," it says. "I noticed how all these spasmodic movements and this continual swaying of his whole body diminished, subsiding by degrees and giving place to a more tranquil attitude." (I recall Truffaut's depiction of this young boy and the way the camera iris closes upon his wet face before the screen fades to black. I want to hold that child, to frame his face with my hands.) And then there is more. "During the night by the beautiful light of the moon, when the rays of this heavenly body penetrated his room," Itard writes, "he rarely failed to awaken and place himself before the window. He stayed there... his neck bent, his eyes fixed upon the moon-lit fields giving himself up to a sort of contemplative ecstasy, the silence and immobility of which were only interrupted at long intervals by deep inspirations nearly always accompanied by a plaintive little sound." In my own reverie, I, too, hear Victor's voice; it is my son's on a restless night. I linger like the governess or Itard near the threshold, listening for Jacob's murmurs to lapse into the comfort of sleep. My mind records the intermingling gestures and babble. I am waiting for something to reveal itself; I want to reveal so much.

And then I turn the corner and descend Dartmouth Street, having circled the neighborhood on my way back home. I pause a moment before I enter the house, looking through the small window of the front door to see Jacob catch the light of the television as he draws on the floor. In my arms, I feel a yearning, the desire to call his name and pull him gently to my chest. When I enter, I sort the finished sketches among the scattered sheets of paper before helping him brush his teeth and wash his face for bed. In his bedroom, I listen as he asks the same question over and over and smiles with satisfaction at the answer that rarely changes, the unvarying script that threatens to diminish a patient tenderness into doubt and despair. Before I go back downstairs, I let the darkness remind me of sleepless nights, the times when I had less of the past to remember and fewer stories to imagine alongside my own—and then I close my eyes and recall all the gentleness that has been and all the moving images that can still be.

III. Layers

THE MELTDOWN

GOODNESS

THE TOWER STORY

The Meltdown

A number of summers ago, when Jacob was nine and Sarah ten, we planned a Sunday afternoon journey to the downtown library. Giving order to the unordered space of a weekend afternoon always seemed an adventure. Would we pack the right portfolio of Jacob's sketches, the Poohs or Madelines or Big Birds? Would we remember the right number of colored pencils for Jacob's drawings and the just-right shade of yellow-orange to color Ernie? Would the library have a copy of the video or book that Jacob had been requesting all morning? Jacob. Jacob. Jacob.

And yet this particular afternoon in mid-June, quiet and brilliant blue, seemed the kind of adventure that left us smiling and acquiescing to Jacob's desires. This day he planned a "photo shoot" of the stuffed storybook characters perched atop the bookshelves in the children's section: the rabbit of Alice's Wonderland, Pooh, a dragon from a story I should know. And so, we searched for the camera and made a special trip to Walgreen's for film and planned enough time to drop off the pictures at Target's one-hour photo. It would be a grand adventure. And, through it all, Sarah laughed and held her brother's hand and entered his vision with all the joy that the hope of one calm day can instill.

The library was not open.

At first, Jacob just wept, letting his shoulders and back hunch forward much like the crying poses of his animated characters—but, quite suddenly, he screamed, ran toward the sliding glass doors, and, strengthened by his anger, nearly forced them open. Sarah stepped forward to try to comfort Jacob, but I warned her back. As we looked on, he began to scratch his face and neck, leaving streaks of red beneath the tender lines of both jaws. For the next ten minutes or so, we coaxed him foot by foot toward and into the van. Once in the back seat, however, he flung himself down and began to kick the windows. I yelled and reached back, grabbing at his shirt and arm. And then he went after Sarah. For a moment, she shrunk back but then she started hitting him and crying and yelling, "I hate you! I hate you!" Finally we opened the door and let his fury back outside. On the sidewalk, Jacob kept lunging toward me, his hands intent upon scratching my face or arms. In the refuge of the van, Sarah called Mary on the cell phone and, in ten minutes, forty-five minutes from the start of his outburst, she pulled up and took Jacob home. His anger now subsiding, he began to sob. "Jacob was so sad," he said. "Jacob was so sad. Jacob was so sad."

My daughter held her own kind of sorrow, and she holds it still. This sorrow has no ritual of completion, no baptism or anointing, no confirmation, no rows of chairs and cheering, no dawn or dusk in which to confess or bear witness. Who will know that in this one hour she held her brother's hand and felt her arms ache to comfort his desperate body, felt her voice tighten and curse, felt her fists against Jacob's chest and back, felt guilt and love and the yearning to begin anew?

I want you to know what no one can know—that the wind caught Sarah's hair and held it off her face for just a moment as she sat next to me on the sidewalk, that she let her small fingers touch the blood on my forearms. I want you to imagine the many things that we leave unspoken, the memories that we must hold in faith because we do not as yet discern their meanings. And I want you to know that Sarah is still reaching out to me and that we do not yet understand the loss instilled in us and the tenacious love that wounds with so much caring.

Goodness

Beneath an umbrella, I watch Sarah from the bleachers. She takes the soccer ball against her right thigh, lets it drop, and, with her right instep, strikes a pass to a teammate and then takes off toward the goal, her pony tail switching the back of her head, her heels flicking off grass and mud. The ball comes back to her; she traps it with her chest. It falls to her feet, but, before she can shoot, the defender bodies up and clears the ball to midfield. She picks herself up from the field and jogs toward the half line. She takes out the band that holds her hair, puts it in her mouth, and quickly performs the ritual of collecting hair between her hands before tying it up again. Her shorts and jersey begin to darken from the rain and cling to the skin. Mud speckles the knees and thighs.

I am watching and writing as I watch, filtering the feel of the cool spring wind and misty rain, converting touch and sight into this endless sprint of images. I am thinking of how much has filled this young life, how much more is to come. I am wondering what she knows; I am wondering how much I can tell.

She remembers that when she was twelve she went bowling at the Western Michigan University student center with Jacob, her friend Mary Kate, and the childcare provider, Lanae. That on their way out after they had finished bowling Jacob noticed a small stage in a banquet hall. That he rushed to the stage and interrupted the people rehearsing, that he refused to leave the room, that he gripped the door jamb and did not let go, that a security officer came and helped drag him outside. That during another trip to the library a security guard had to take him out after he had begun screaming because a video was not on the shelf. That the man said he would call the police if he did not leave. That Jacob immediately grew quiet, remembering the Curious George story about when he accidentally called in a fire alarm and was taken to jail. That for years Jacob would always talk to the security guard, confusing pronouns in the pleading, "He will be good. He will be good." Sarah remembers that one summer, after Jacob tried to hit her, Lanae told him he cannot hurt his sister. That another babysitter told her to go downstairs with her friend, Brigid, away from his anger and that, from the basement, she could hear him throwing things and yelling, "Sarah, help me, please! Help me, please!"

I can picture her sitting upon the bottom steps, motionless, obedient. I can see how her left forearm and elbow lean against the higher step, how her chest moves in and out, how the muffled thuds and urgent calls rumble through her limbs. I can envision her imagining all the possibilities in the midst of this captive feeling: the hero's coming upon the scene and translating the language of rage into calmness and understanding, the martyr's self-denial, the acceptance of scratches and teeth, the purging that comes in sacrifice and surrender. I can see a dancer's balance in the way Sarah's thigh and calf tense as if ready to run across a stage, her body motionless beneath the cacophony of upstairs footsteps. I can hear what she wants to call out. "It's all right, Jacob. It's okay. It's all right. It's okay." What does it mean to live in the place that freezes the desire to spring up the steps, that suspends the potential to heal and to save? What is this spectator life, this still life of inner churning, this off stage and understudy existence?

Can I offer my own rememberings alongside hers? When I was seven, I went to see my dying grandmother, the one from Liverpool who married my American grandfather during the First World War and traveled back with him to his home in Lakeside, Iowa. Less stern than my maternal grandmother, she spoiled us with dollar bills in birthday cards. In her cottage, my sisters and I felt like Little Red

Riding Hood's siblings, carrying little gifts without the threat of a wolf. Over the backs of chairs, she threw the web of cross-stitched doilies. From a cedar chest, she pulled cardboard images of London and Paris, of the rose windows in French cathedrals, and slipped them into the stereoscope. We looked through the binocular-like eye pieces, watching the distant places come magically into focus. She told us Grimms' fairy tales, the ones about luck and wit and sacrifice. At the hospital, my father sat in a chair near the bed as my youngest sister and I played with a wind-up Christmas angel that turned round and round to "Silent Night"; my grandmother's thin, empty body frightened us. She called out to us from the bed, the same inviting storyteller's voice but now with witch's hands.

In the funeral home, her casket gaped open in the back near the church entrance. I remember the long walk from the front of the church to my father. I looked up into his face as it broke into weeping. I wanted to be so good; I held his hand and did not cry, even when my own gut cringed at his trembling mouth and strange sobs, even when grief shook off the mask of fatherhood and revealed unfamiliar flesh. Who was the son now? Who the father? I wonder how long I stood watching before we walked back to the pew, away from the cedar scent of his mother's sweater. I wonder how much I allowed him to be a son, to remember the touch of her hand in his, before I gently tugged his fingers. What did it mean to hold my face father-like before my grandmother's son? What was this compassion that knocks like a wolf at the cottage door, this devouring love that accompanies grief and suffering and the unwelcome sacrifices of childhood?

After we returned home, I sat in my room, waiting, certain of only my yearning for goodness. I can hear the steps and floorboards giving way to the weight of my mother's footsteps. She walks the hallway between the slant of the ceiling wall and stair well. She is young, just thirty-seven in this remembering. When she sits beside me on the bed, her head does not nod with age, the backs of her hands do not show blood-filled veins fraying around knuckles. She holds me and lets me weep.

I make out what the boy cannot recall or did not yet know.

That his legs tremble in the sharp angle of afternoon sunlight. That outside the lilac bushes scratch at the winter wind. That against the curb the snow glistens as it melts then freezes into clusters of ice. That the wet snow slides off the leafless limbs of oak and ash. That this beautiful unburdening explains the stark design of unbending things. And I know what my mother does not say. That she feels goodness in the waves of his chest against hers. That she seeks the name for the tide of this compassion. I know what she prays but may not always believe, the truths that spread out, unwelcoming, like flat land in January: that winter barrenness is grace, that frost only goes so deep, that goodness is the traveling seed blown from the stem, a slender shoot that hurries from the split kernel caught in spring mud.

My daughter knows the world through a different remembering. She knows mornings through the endless play of Disney songs, knows all Disney or Pixar movie scripts by heart, having sat upon the couch or in the car as Jacob watched *Aladdin* or *Toy Story* or *101 Dalmatians* or *A Bug's Life* hundreds of times. She knows that meaning sometimes must be caught in the absurd ways that Jacob echoes video phrases and performs the various masks of sadness or anger or surprise in the mirror. She understands that, when we return home in the van from soccer games, she can prop a pillow against his shoulder or upon his lap and sleep. She knows that he will wait out her resting until his legs grow numb. She sees that she is one of three people who understands the verbs and nouns of his idiosyncratic speech, the secrets encoded in the unique mesh of experience and memory. She carries the weight of this intimate knowing as if she were the last storyteller. She feels as if she must break open at times with the fullness of unspoken expectations. She mothers, provokes, resents, embraces, laments, and laughs. At night, from her room, she shuts her door to the loud noise of her brother's "laughing alert." She calls out to him to be quiet, calls down to us to ask him to be quiet. And, sometimes, she laughs at each plentiful outburst, slipping her legs between the sheets and quilt, perhaps surrendering to the comforting rootedness of just how much she can know and still love.

When people ask and settle in to listen, she will tell how Jacob disrobes when he goes to the bathroom, tossing his socks, sweat pants, and underwear on the floor just like the little boy in the children's book *Everyone Poops*. She laughs at once having feared playing Bert to Jacob's Ernie on Halloween. She accepts without embarrassment that many of her high school friends have seen him naked, heard him say "Fire in the hole!" and then pass gas.

But, inevitably, she drifts toward memories that remain vivid in how faces break into anger or sudden remorse or grief. Standing on Fifth Avenue in New York, she watches Jacob read the sign on the door of the Disney Store: "We are closing at 7:30 this evening. Sorry for the inconvenience." "If they only knew," she must think, backing toward the curb and surveying the scene as Jacob takes in the meaning. She watches a twenty-something woman turn after hearing Jacob shout at the worker behind the glass door, "I will hit him. I will hit him." Even on the busy street, space opens up around the drama. In her hand, she holds the bag of newly-purchased clothes from H & M; she can only think, "How unlucky is that. The Disney Store closes at 7:30 on the last night in the city that never sleeps." If they had not reverently sat for an extra few minutes at St. Patrick's Cathedral they might have gotten into the store. Jacob had even lit a candle, no doubt to the gods of Disney and the patron saints of Ariel and Cinderella. She laughs. It is a story, after all, full of dark humor and irony.

I have to tell one last story. It is another kind of goodness, this desire to prepare the field together, to turn over winter-packed soil and let the clods of dirt fall unevenly, to let the spade drop and break the sod, mixing together the different layers of our pasts. It is rough work, this tilling.

Listen. I had been playing basketball for years. My young life centered around the next pick up game in a driveway or, as I got older, at the local YMCA or Buena Vista College athletic center. (As a high school senior, I often joined friends on Sunday pleading with the local Y director for the gym key.) Since third grade, when my home town team won the state basketball tournament, I had competed hard for a starting position on any team, attended countless summer camps, and endured weeks of pre-season conditioning and the fear of throwing up. I dreamed intensely of winning the state basketball title, of playing in Des Moines Veteran's Auditorium, of seeing my team in the tournament programs, of hearing friends and family talk of staying home to watch the game on television or traveling to the capital. Starting in high school, I rarely missed a week without shooting baskets; for years, I had a heat blister on my small toes, red and calloused. When I was not playing basketball, I was watching it on television or imagining all the endless possibilities of final heroics.

In these imaginings, I drew from the adrenaline of real experiences, the time when I converted a last second shot and felt the crowd flow on the court and around my body as I jumped up and down. I remembered the feel of my muscles when pivoting, the moments that athletes experience in the zone, the fluidity between the movement of the body and the mindful willing of the sudden sprint, pull up, and shot, the state of suspension when action slows and the crowd senses something beautiful and flowing, feels joy in their own bodies, the releasing. I knew what it meant to let myself surrender. I did not know what comes after the last game. I had not imagined the possibility.

Here is what happened. We were ranked in the top ten in our division. We won our way to the substate final, the last game before Des Moines. With fifteen seconds left, we had a point lead. The other team brought the ball down the court, passed it to their best shooter, who missed badly. As I glanced quickly toward the clock, the last second ticked off; within the space of that glance and the noise of the buzzer, I tensed my body to jump in celebration, then saw the opposing guard scoop the ball towards the basket with two hands. The ball banked in.

I returned home, emptied out. My mother and father sat at the east end of the living room beneath a circle of lamp light. I collapsed in a chair beneath the west window, put my hands to my face, and began to say how it had all been for nothing. I kept thinking of the inexplicability of that last shot, how it violated the angles of trajectory, how the shooter had no time for intention or aim or form. He was a random body moved to a point of contact, an orbit of limbs fated for this one outcome. Even now, I am surprised by how deeply I felt the arbitrary finality of the act, how quickly the loss broke the tenor of my voice, how the past seemed to tumble away now, uprooted.

My father came to me and knelt at my side. He took my right hand between his palms and held it. His thick fingers, creased with paint from his auto body shop, warmed my knuckles.

I want now to let my hands and arms enfold all that he saw in this young man's body: eyes and lips wet with grief, a face unknowing of the vast stretch of loss, just glimpsing the fissures that open along things that change. I want to be his hand upon the knee. I want his tenderness when the fields open up for the next rain. I want the goodness that memory shoots into the limbs, the goodness of arms and of earth.

I am back in the bleachers, watching through the lens of memory, cultivating the past, turning the packed soil and creating gaps in the spring sod, the spaces that catch and hold seeds, the ones newly thawed and drifting, urgent to split and take root.

The soccer game nears the last minute. In the van at the north end of the field, Mary watches at a distance, running the heat and wipers as Jacob draws. I see the van from the stands and measure the separation between all of us, the need to watch from afar or to wait for the retelling or to dig up memories and compose what might have been missed or simply what might have been.

My daughter falls and rises again, gulping air like a replenishing sadness. I watch the quick stride of her legs, the way a foot plants before she pivots, how her shoulder dips into a defender's forearm. I can feel the goodness in all her movement, seen and unseen, in the weariness that comes from straining through the weight of rain and mud, in the joyful releasing of legs and of love, in the longing for the last bruise to heal before the next blow buds.

THE TOWER STORY

Just beyond the backyard fence alongside our neighbor's yard, a tall metal windmill rises between a thick oak tree and spindly cedars. Near a farm grove, it would not be out of place; in fact, coming from rural Iowa, I think of the wooden windmills that used to draw water for livestock. From the highway, these decaying towers can sometimes be seen at the edge of groves long cleared of farm houses and machine sheds. At times, they may stand along a distant fence line, the brown sun of the upper fan immobile in the wind. The neighbor's windmill is an odd sight, then: appropriate to flat Midwest landscapes, not tree-lined city neighborhoods. The story that we tell, one first narrated to us by the son of the past owner, is that the windmill served as a ham radio tower. At its top, antennas still crisscross the sky, forming a haphazard alphabet against a backdrop of clouds, cables dangling down the metal trunk.

Since both Sarah and Jacob grew up with a desire to climb things, Mary and I have spent many hours worrying about the tower. My fears only increased when, one afternoon not long after moving onto the street, the neighbor's oak tree lost a large limb during a storm and collapsed part of the fence. For a few weeks, entrance into their yard required only a little maneuvering through thick oak branches. One day, Jacob finally strayed over to the tower. I watched him stretch his arms toward the lowest cross bar before hurrying to retrieve him. In the weeks before the fence was fixed, we monitored his movements vigilantly, expecting at some point, having lost track of his whereabouts, to look out the kitchen window and see him all the way at the top.

Over the years, the tower has been a central feature in a variety of stories that I tell myself about Sarah and her brother. Some are heroic; some are tragic. In all of my anxious make-believe, rooted in actual news accounts of kids who wandered away, Sarah calls for us when she notices that Jacob has ascended to the top, but Mary and I are absent. She runs to the tower and climbs, the wind threading its hollow voice through the trees. Amid the angled bars of the last section, Jacob balances like Winnie-the-Pooh. He pretends to be a rain cloud, stretching his arm toward the sky, balloon in hand, threatening to release himself toward the highest branch of the nearby oak. Sarah extends her fingers toward him, striving to interrupt the dangerous play.

It is hard work living with such stories.

Here is the heroic version of the tale.

"Remember," Sarah coaxes, "Pooh could float. You can't"

Jacob stops balancing on one foot. "The wrong sorts of bees," he laughs.

My daughter continues her flawless Pooh logic: "Besides, he was made of fluff and stuff. When he fell, he bounced from branch to branch and did not get hurt. He is just a Disney character. He is pretend." Sarah is fluent in Pooh.

The neighbors gather as she balances between the soft-edged world of Pooh and Curious George and the unbending reality of hard bars, sharp angles, and the pull of gravity. In her pidgin language, a cross between Disney video-speak and real-world vocabulary, she translates the dangers, telling him to wait for Christopher Robin's friends. She calms him with reminders that even Curious George could not let go of his balloons when floating so high above the city buildings, that the Man with the Yellow Hat had to pluck him from the air. She moves to his side, curls fingers from her right hand in his belt loop, and twists a loose cable around her left arm, binding herself to her brother and the tower. She finds a way to suspend the fear and thinks. In her mind, she recalls the climbing toys in the Tot Lot near family friends. She hears Marion call her name: "Sarah. Sarah. Let go and slide down." But, then, she stops remembering, breaks from the recollection just before Marion's arms take her in. Such reverie has consequences when sitting so far up with her brother.

Shading their eyes as they look up, the neighbors see the intertwined silhouette of Sarah and Jacob. Against the bright sky beyond the tower's peak, the two blend into a shade of black like the muddied Pooh of Milne's book before the mess dripped down the white pages. Eventually, I imagine Jacob letting Sarah guide him down. When his feet touch the ground, he dashes away. He runs from the wrong sorts of bees, runs from storybook firemen, runs laughing as Pooh and George spin their happy endings through his imagination. People take turns congratulating Sarah. This is the Curious George version of the tower story, the one where curiosity never falls into the fist of the earth.

The tower story represents an archetypal fear for many families who have a child with autism. Alongside the tales of runners from home who drown in a nearby pond or swimming pool or get lost in a forest on vacation, the water or electric or radio tower tales are more than autist-urban legends in the minds of parents and siblings.

One of the most compelling true stories happened to John McNeil and his seventeen-year old brother, James, on February 11, 1997 in Mesa, Arizona. The initial Associated Press report offered the critical facts: "A 10-year-old autistic boy and his teen-age brother spent two hours Tuesday atop a 120-foot-tall electrical tower before rescue crews got them down… The tower carries 230,000-volt power from lines for the Salt River Project, which cut off electricity to allow crews to reach the boys with a crane." According to the press release, the local television stations "skipped the national evening newscast to broadcast the rescue as it was happening." CBS *This Morning* picked up the story the next day, introducing an interview with Captain Terry Self, the firefighter who was first to get to the boys, with the dramatic lead, "An Arizona boy is safe this morning thanks to the heroic efforts of his teen-age brother and a dramatic rescue." "It's just amazing," Self said, "that these two boys were able to get up there and then for us to get them back down without them getting hurt."

Photos and video clips began to accompany the newspaper and television coverage. In Wednesday's *The Seattle Times*, AP photos showed John and James atop the tower as well as an "after" shot of the mother, Saundra McNeil, comforting her youngest son. From *The Seattle Times* to the *Hamilton Spectator* in Ontario to the *Scottish Daily Record* (Headline: "High There Bruv, Grins Pylon Kid"), the image of the boys on the tower served as verbal and visual shorthand for the heroic script. That John had autism magnified the scope of the danger and the poignance of James's stiff vigil. Two bound figures against the horizon, the younger oblivious to the older's sacrifice.

Not surprisingly, the brief, factual reporting gives way to the desire to piece together a larger story, to provide an uplifting narrative to soften up the hard news of the day or week. On May 6, *Dateline NBC* includes the segment: "Terror in the Tower." Moving to the show's "Survivor Story" profile, Jane Pauley opens, "Sure you love your brothers and sisters. You'd go to the ends of the earth for them. Then how about 120 feet straight up? That was the decision facing an extraordinary brave young man you're about to meet tonight, and he didn't think twice about it." In the segment itself, Keith Morrison introduces the family and, through the interplay of photographs, video, interviews, and voiceover, shows what John's autism meant to him and his family:

> **Ms. McNeil:** He's outgoing. He's friendly. He's warm and affectionate. He's a good artist.
> **Morrison:** He simply expresses himself in ways that are different from other kids.
> **Ms. McNeil:** Yeah! Often unexpected. That's why I feel it's like having a two-year-old forever.
> **Morrison:** Mm-hmmm.
> **Mr. B. McNeil:** You know that as much as we would like, he's probably not going to become a brain surgeon. He's probably not going to go to college. So we have to make sure, as much as

possible, that we take care of his needs.

Morrison: (Voiceover) And provide for his safety, because John is fearless and has a knack for getting into sticky situations.

(John running out of house and away from his mother)

Ms. McNeil: You're not funny.

He has thrilled lots of play yard supervisors by climbing to the top of the jungle gym and standing there and flapping his arms and not holding on.

Morrison: (Voiceover) That's why the family must carefully choose where they settle.

(McNeil family photo)

Ms. McNeil: It has to be a place without a pool, without tall trees, and not near a canal, or near a busy street.

It turns out that the nearby towers that John saw through his bedroom window repeatedly drew him outside. Prior to the climb on February 11, he had escaped to the tower a number of times, making it as high as thirty feet on one occasion before being coaxed down.

In the November 1997 *Reader's Digest*, William Hendryx offered another profile of James McNeil, adding a few more details while still following *Dateline's* formula. We learn that, when James arrived at the tower, John was only eighteen feet high, that he refused to attend to James's commands to climb down, that James "heard the electricity coursing through the thick, insulated wires nearby," a transfer of power that "sounded like a hornet's nest." We read that James snagged his shorts and then nearly fell at the next bolt step and that, at the very top, "grabbed John's left wrist in a death grip," asked him to move over, and wrapped "his legs around the diagonal support brace" to anchor himself. (In the *Dateline* interview, Terry Self recalled that when he picked up James's hand, the grip had been so tight that "his brother's hand was blue.") We hear that the half-dozen news helicopters circling the tower led John to wave his right hand excitedly, causing James to further tighten his hold on his brother's wrist. And, in the long attendance at the top of the tower, we learn that James distracted his brother and calmed himself by singing a favorite hymn again and again until his voice grew raw:

I am a child of God,
And he has sent me here;
He's given me an earthly home,
with parents kind and dear.

The McNeil story airs occasionally on cable, packaged in a show featuring remarkable rescues caught on video. Once, as I was clicking from cable channel to channel, I paused as the program cut to the electrical tower. To my surprise, I saw the brothers. Beneath the helicopter filming the scene hovered another. The electric company truck, hurriedly repaired to get to the site, raised its one-hundred fifty foot arm. When the piece ended, I sat numbly on the couch. I imagined how James's stomach must have felt, sitting as if stuck in the first car of a roller coaster at the ride's peak, ten stories high, his body continually anticipating the breathless descent. I thought of the kind of loyalties and loves that lead to such high-wire vigils—and then felt the sudden emotional knowing. I understood what James McNeil meant when he said he did not understand the fuss, as if climbing toward his brother was a choice. To the *Dateline* reporter, here is what James replied when asked about living with John: "It may be a little trialsome at times, but I have a really wonderful brother, usually... [Voiceover] And I love him."

We need to be witness to such unconditional love. But, even if uttered in humor, how might we understand the "usually" that comes between the wonderful brother and this love? The voiceover hovers like a refrain, an echo that can only be fully appreciated if the listener imagined the time atop the tower and felt all that the body must take in: the hornet buzz threatening an electric sting, the raw taste of a church hymn scratching the throat, the concussion of helicopter blades pounding the air.

What, then, is the nature of this heroism, this surrender of self? In these media accounts of the hero tale, what gets overlooked? Whose yearnings are not fully expressed when the medals get handed out? Can a word or just one story encompass the tower feeling, or can this kind of love only be understood in a recycling of the core tale itself?

Being constantly on guard does not always lead to such high plac-es; it may only end in a simple embarrassed stumbling or running away. Less dramatic events take place on the ground, sometimes with a sudden search and discovery, sometimes with a ducking for cover.

In August of 2008, we moved Sarah from home to Ann Arbor to start her first year at the University of Michigan. Atop the van, we stacked pre-cut lumber for two bed lofts; behind the middle seat, we squeezed an apartment-sized refrigerator, computer printer, school supplies, detergent and softener for a term, and enough clothes to ride out the fashion demands of first classes and parties. The logis-tics of the day also involved packing for Jacob: sufficient drawing supplies, a DVD player, a stack of DVDs, a walkman and tapes, and, of course, two bags stuffed with old drawings, notebooks of xeroxes, books, and favorite magazines. In other words, it was a normal trip for Jacob; it was an extraordinary time for Sarah, a threshold mo-ment for her—and for all of us.

In the months before Sarah's move-in day, Mary and I talk-ed about whether we both could go. The first half of the year had been especially difficult for Jacob. His sixteen-year-old frustrations had led to more frequent moments of aggression; in fact, we had met with a crisis team through the local district, developed a list of ready supports (including a first-responder number at the Crisis Center), even learned techniques to deflect his physical lunges. We had talked about how to give him more freedom, to honor his desire for independence without taking away the scaffolding of necessary schedules and verbal directions. In these early years of adolescence, we understood that our listening to Jacob, as always, involved taking into account his behaviors as much as his words. And, of course, we also knew that he had begun processing the fact that Sarah would soon be gone: no more soccer trips, less frequent times for eating out "with Sarah," and fewer laughing alerts or duets. "We're a duo, a DUO"—one of Jacob's and Sarah's favorite songs from *An American Tale*—would not enter the chaotic evenings of two showers and pre-sleep movie watching.

In the end, we arranged for someone to stay with Jacob at home so that we could attend to all the work and worry of the move—and to grant Sarah a rare occasion of our own undivided attention. But, in the previous week, the arrangements fell through. So, with some trepidation, we approached the day not unlike past soccer tournaments. For me, an initial sadness over the need to split attention again gave way to another feeling: an excitement in building the lofts for Sarah and her roommate, an anticipation of seeing the newness of this experience light up my daughter's eyes, and, yes, a satisfaction of having us all be a part of the ritual and its shared memories.

We knew the dangers. If Mary or I were not clear with who "had" Jacob, we risked his wandering off, perhaps to search for videos or DVDs in an open room or ride the elevator down to another floor. Years before, when we got caught up tiling our kitchen floor, we received a call from a neighbor friend a block up the street just as we realized Jacob was gone. "Are you missing anyone?" Tom joked. "Jacob is in our TV room looking through videos." Such full-day affairs, then, called for a disciplined vigilance and hyper-awareness, a kind of tag-team approach that assured us all that someone would be watching or running interference. And, of course, Sarah had to be one of the watchers.

In the week before the trip, Mary spent time reminding Jacob of helpful conversation rules. If his innocent and undiscriminating naming of places and people colored anew our own interpretation of the world ("That awning is like Sesame Street!" or "You have grey hair; you are a grandmother!"), it also risked exchanges not easily explained to strangers. Having watched the teenage rap singer Lil' Bow Wow in the movie *Like Mike*, he would occasionally call kids at the city bus terminal Lil' Bow Wow. In light of these experiences, Mary and I rehearsed the rules whenever we had the opportunity: Remember that we do not talk about how people look! We do not talk about other people's bodies! Home is the place to talk about private things. (The list of private things got bigger: weight, diapers, physical handicaps, baldness.)

In addition to his curiosity about and excessive concern for people in wheelchairs or on crutches or with missing limbs, Jacob's newest curiosity was differences in skin color, a preoccupation that led to a trip to Hobby Lobby to purchase a range of skin-tone colored pencils. And, once we said that Lil' Bow Wow was black, he desired comparable categories for all the people he was beginning to see through a different verbal lens: Mexican Americans, Asian Americans, and, because we were of a distinct color as well, European Americans. Through Jacob's questions, we were hearing again the incompleteness of our country's racial and ethnic vocabulary.

Just before lunch time, I heard Sarah and Mary call Jacob's name in the hallway. Having begun building the lofts, I had turned intently to sorting the sections, matching posts, bolts, and bed slats, and, along with the roommate's mother, assembling the various parts. Some time elapsed, then, before I realized that Sarah and Mary were no longer on the floor. They returned with Jacob; he had gotten curious and taken the elevator down to the lobby level. They arrived at the main floor just as he was about to turn down a corridor to the lobby of the residential hall. Apparently, he was looking for a rest-room—and, perhaps, seeking the table of donuts and juice that greet-ed us in the morning. Sarah discovered him, his right hand nimbly clicking the rewind button on his walkman, earphones scratching out some Disney video tune, a quick turn away from where our imaginations did not want to go: his sudden recognition that he was lost, his urgent calls, "Mom, where are you? Sarah? Sarah?", and his inability to provide information to find his way back.

And the move had other moments. When returning from lunch, we approached a family coming from Sarah's wing of the residential hall. "Hi, African Americans," Jacob called, waving his hand. Ahead of us, we saw our daughter dash up the steps as we ap-proached our son with a gentle reminder not to talk about people. Returning to the seventh floor, a young African American woman got on the elevator with us just before the door closed. She had a room not far down the hall from Sarah.

"We can only talk about African Americans at home," Jacob thought aloud.

Sometimes we can know what to expect through other well-told, tower stories. A few years ago, when Sarah was just entering high school, I happened across an early 1990s film that anticipated the outer and inner truths of these sibling realities. In *What's Eating Gilbert Grape*, Johnny Depp plays Gilbert, the oldest brother in a family of five profoundly affected by a younger brother whose echolalic speech and inappropriate social behaviors have led some viewers to place him on the autism spectrum. In addition to dealing with Arnie (acted with striking nuance and humanity by Leonardo DiCaprio, who received an Academy Award nomination for the role), the family carries the burden of their father's suicide and, quite literally, the mother's weight. A former beauty queen, she now weighs over five hundred pounds and refuses to leave the house. (The only time that she ventures from her home is when Arnie is jailed for repeatedly climbing the rural Iowa town's water tower.) While centering as much on the disabling impact of the mother's weight as on the constant need to supervise her youngest son, the film can still be read as a parable of constantly needing to be on watch. With the family, we witness isolating allegiances and desperate betrayals that arise within a house that has succumbed to the sometimes chaotic churning of unconditional love.

While Arnie constantly seeks to climb trees and water towers, his siblings strive to keep the house from falling in upon itself. For Gilbert especially, the effort results in a kind of emotional paralysis. Much has gone into shoring up this precarious household. Beneath the living room couch that holds the mother, the family has had to insert additional beams to brace the floor joists. And, in the endless daily routines, Gilbert escorts his brother to town, gives him his bath, and puts him to bed—as his sisters take on the burden of housework and Arnie's approaching birthday party. It is Gilbert who ultimately accepts the primary responsibility of caring for his brother. When he works at the small downtown family grocery store, he keeps Arnie with him. And, whether having lunch with friends or ice cream with Becky (a visitor to the town played by Juliette Lewis), Gilbert must keep constant watch over Arnie's desire to escape and climb the water tower. The cost of a momentary distraction or desire is the hard reality of hearing his brother's voice call down from nearly three stories high.

In this tower story, then, Gilbert has learned to deny personal yearnings, leaving his emotional life as lightly stocked as the grocery store inventory. Between his mother's immobility and his brother's constant demands, he sinks into a routine of laboring with others' wants and not his own. Even with a local housewife's repeated delivery requests (and ensuing attempts at sexual play), he seems less passionate than accommodating. If at first there was mutual pleasure, we enter the film at a time when Gilbert has let himself become just a part of the delivery. He accepts but does not seem capable of naming or asserting his own wants. He climbs when he must but only for Arnie; within all the chaos and absurdity of his life, he appears to see this sacrifice as his saving virtue. As his friendship grows with Becky, however, he faces questions that begin to bring this emptiness to the surface:

> Becky: Tell me what you want as fast as it comes to you…. Okay.
> Gilbert: Okay.
> Becky: Okay, what do you want? [Pause] Faster…
> Gilbert: I want a new thing. House. I want a new house for the family. I want Momma to take aerobics classes. I want Ellen to grow up. I want a new brain for Arnie. I want…
> Becky: What do you want for you…just for you?
> Gilbert: [Pause] I want to be a good person. [Pause] I can't…I can't do this. I can't….
> Becky: Okay.
> Gilbert: Where's Arnie?

As with other moments, the penalty for not devoting undivided attention to his brother is another crisis: Arnie's successful trek to the top of the tower. This time, after being rescued with the help of a large crane, the local police roughly take the boy away and lock him up. Here is the felt reality of Gilbert's life: to pause and speak from personal longings, to open up to the feeling so that it can be named, risks hurting the person who he has most protected. Thinking of himself only threatens to negate or blemish a redemptive selflessness. Later, when his frustration peaks during the wearisome routine of bath time, Gilbert strikes Arnie and leaves the house. Though unexpected in its cruelty, it also releases what Gilbert must have long held inside: the desire to act in anger, to bring on the full force of retribution, and to make so much unseen turmoil visible. It is too simple to call his behavior self-destructive; rather, it is an odd and spontaneous creation, filled simultaneously with self-loathing and the struggle to articulate a deep, abiding self-worth. His rage is a way to see the outlines of some hidden core, to feel again his inner self.

As viewers, as those outside looking in or beneath the tower looking up, we come to understand how anger can reside alongside such tenderness and sacrifice. We glimpse why the sibling wishes to deny so much. What does it mean, after all, to let desire be reawakened in a life with so much sacrifice? What does it mean to live in a place where the floor joists and makeshift beams hold up what needs to fall down and be rebuilt? If goodness only prevails by endlessly beating back private wants, by seemingly always attending to someone else first, then even the most generous giving must at times seem false and insincere to the giver. How, then, does the weight get lifted without forsaking the full range of needs, without the abuse of others or oneself? How does one live with the tower when the cameras have pulled away the rescue ladders?

No one is served by stories that wrap courage and sacrifice so tightly around love, that make the heroic moment or gesture the only truth. Such tales bind brothers and sisters, the ones who climb and the ones who follow, to an inevitable fall.

For this falling, after all, is the twin tale of the heroic tower story, a plot that replaces feet on the earth with a deathlike plunging, an ending rooted in doubt and despair and an obsessive lingering upon unsought sacrifices.

Here is one version that I keep imagining, one that follows the descending arc of Gilbert Grape's struggles. This story has no children's-book logic, no Christopher Robin or Man in the Yellow Hat, no softness to catch the fall of Jacob's fantasizing, no shared songs and final embraces. The metal bars are cold to the touch; the arches of the feet ache with each step up the ladder. In my imagination, Sarah climbs and calls to Jacob and then to anyone who might hear.

No one calls back or comes to the foot of the tower. Jacob holds on to the top rung with only one hand; in the other, he grips a helium balloon. Just before she reaches his feet, he slips. She sees the surprise on his face, almost like the breathlessness that pulls the head back when swinging too high or when the roller coaster begins its descent. And then the sound, the muffled breaking, the escape of breath, the screaming and the sirens, the wailing that gives way to whispers, silence, and then the burdensome absence of Jacob's running and climbing and hitting and laughing and the endless rewinding of it all.

I wonder what compels me to make up this story. Against all that has shaped my own vigilance, against the ever-present desire to build fences to protect Sarah and Jacob, why do I strip the narrative of the chain link and door locks? Why do I invite the imagination to sicken the heart? And why put Sarah on the ladder? Why must she be the witness? Is it because the possibility exists as long as the windmill rises in the neighbor's yard, that there is always a tower somewhere?

Perhaps I am narrating this story because it takes me to another emotional place, to a part of the sibling story that I have been leaving out, the episodes that threaten estrangement instead of reconciliation, a leaving rather than a hopeful return or acceptance of flaws and failures. To capture this important scene in the plot I must enter as a character and see myself through Sarah's eyes—and my son's. It is another bath time episode but without Depp or DiCaprio. And it is definitely not the tape that rolls on the soft news of *Dateline*.

Cut away to Mary and me preparing for a trip to the beach. We take out the digital camera and begin to delete pictures that we have already saved on our computer. We come to one of me, without my glasses. For a moment, I do not recognize myself. I do not understand this face: lips pressed together, eyes staring intently at the camera. I am not posing for anything even as I clearly know something is being taken. And then I recall the instant of this imprint, this flash in time. And I see what my son has seen and will continue to witness vividly in his memories of our lives together.

It starts at 8 pm.

"Time to take a shower," I say.

Jacob revels in TV free time, the space in the day when he has unlimited access to the replaying of videos and DVDs. It is a sacred time, one he aggressively protects.

"Do not give me choices. No choices."

I repeat the choice, evenly, trying to empty my voice of anger and anxiety. I am unsuccessful.

"We can do the shower now or at 8:15."

"Dad is repeating," he says, raising the pitch at the "ing"; "Dad is repeating."

I no longer have spoken language now. So, I put words on a piece of paper and slide it on the shelf in front of him, atop the *Christmas Eve on Sesame Street* video and the open *Charlotte's Web* DVD case. "Shower at 8:15," it says.

At 8:15, Jacob is still playing a section of the Sesame Street video along with a cassette music mix. I come to the cassette player and turn it off. I reach toward the television on/off button and push. "Shower time," I say.

In his eyes, I see that he will come toward me; I know he will scratch my hands, that he will pinch the underside of my upper arm. He has learned how to use my movement against me, how to find the vulnerable places on my body, so I go into the bedroom and get a sweatshirt to wear. It is summer and warm in the house, but I want to avoid the later pain of scratch marks. As I leave the room, I hear him throwing the couch cushions. He runs into the kitchen, leaps into the air, pounds his feet on the tile floor. The pizza pan on the oven rattles. Our dog Gypsy threads her way toward the basement door; she seeks the dark place between the desk and futon downstairs.

"If you break things or hurt me, I will hold you down." The words now begin to sound like a taped message.

I begin to feel my adrenaline pump as I spread my legs to have a firm base, a solid balance, like a sprinter tensing for a key exchange of weight and motion before the starter's gun or a football lineman ready to come out of his crouch to absorb the rush.

No one else is in the house. No one. Just Jacob and I, and I feel the risk in this isolation.

"Stay back," I say, but now my voice is uneven. My anger and desperation mix together. As he strikes me, I know how close I am to hurting Jacob, and I begin to wonder if I needed to get to this place, if I could have waited longer. I move about the room as Jacob tries to get hold of me; I strive to stay outside his reach for five minutes, ten minutes, fifteen, moving the last of the most fragile items from the room. But, after he head butts me on the chin and lip as I try to hold him, I push him too hard against his back, and he falls to the floor.

It is all over then. He topples chairs, kicks at my legs. He gets the camera from the other room. "I'll flash you," he yells, and then he does aim it at me like a weapon from *Star Wars* and pushes the button. He cries, "Dad pushed me! Dad hit me!" It is a righteous screaming, bitter, and distraught—and I know that he is just in his rage. Even worse, his words sound to me as if they come from behind the boy whose face seems to betray only anger and the desire to hurt, the boy caught, too, in a body and mind that at times cannot stop once the gun fires. He can only hurtle toward some tenuous endpoint and wait to feel the tape against the chest, some signal to let up or let go, some purging that we both endure.

But this is not the whole story. Often, there has been someone else in the house: Sarah. Over the years, she has seen the flash of my face tight with anger. She has confronted my impatient dismissals of her tenacious effort to help or intervene, seemingly powerless to change what has happened or to understand her own heroic or stubborn desire to stand and watch, a desire that will accept the mark of such memories because it seems the only way to embrace the players on the stage.

Here, then, is the dilemma. What kind of story can mediate the pull toward the dramatic extremes of sacrifice and bitterness, of the exhilaration of coming down intact and the constant tension of an impending crisis? In the actual lived experience, in the hidden intimacies and conflicts of the home, how can the brother and brother, sister and sister, brother and sister live with a sense of incessant watchfulness? Though there may not be a tower next door, the vigilance remains inside, a furnace pilot light ready to fire. It exists in conjunction with all the small transitions, obsessions, and potential ruptures in any day: a calm sketching suddenly crumpled into pinching when a colored pencil tip breaks, a spontaneous after-noon nap transformed into an evening's anxiety when "we missed 3 o'clock." For Sarah, the signs of potential breakages are present in the inventory on the shelves and in the closets: replacement VCRs, Walkmans, 90-minute audio cassette tapes, and fine tip pens for the old and over-used things when they lose their buttons or sound or black ink. But for some moments there are no replacements, no in-terventions: the power unexpectedly going out during peak usage in August or after a car accident topples an electric pole, the special-ty shoelace snapping in the fingers without the remedy of an open store. This cadence of living can feel like a perpetual loss of order and calm—for the sister, certainly, but also for a brother enduring these uncertainties in a world of too much talk and too many demands. It is a persistent cutting off of all that cultivates the illusion of uninter-rupted joy or soft conversation and quiet laughter. Even when the breeze is calm and tone of voice sweet like the wild roses stitched within our neighbor's fence, we know that a front may move through and peel the limb from the trunk—and the beauty of Jacob's peculiar codes and coloring of the world can be forgotten in an unforgiving weariness. The sibling parable is the rhythm of willing and imposed patience, vigilance and selflessness, and the uneasy expectation of unanticipated loss.

Can you come to this place where my daughter stands? Can you, too, learn to be carried out into the rough sea of it, the place where the imagination and muscles must accommodate the uneven-ness and fluidity, the small waves and large, the crest and fall? This is why people keep telling stories, to give some scope to the place in which they find themselves, the latitude and longitude—even when the storm seems years away or impossible in the momentary calm.

Who must we be? Who must we become to be able to live with the cadence of this rise and fall?

Before these more recent years of striving to understand my daughter's life, I remember reading my first sibling story. It was in the back of a thick, authoritative research text addressing all the dimensions of autism: diagnosis, language, social interactions, and more. Concluding the book were four first-person narratives: an essay by a parent, by a teacher, by Temple Grandin, one of the most well-known people on the autism spectrum, and a piece by Jason Konidaris, a twenty-something sibling looking back on his family years. In his recollections, he brings forth one of the archetypal moments of the sibling experience: the loss of his brother. Having left the front door unlocked, his brother wandered off, leaving Konidaris to face the questions of his panicked parents: "Who left the front door open? How long was it open? Where is he? He's gone. Jason, did you leave the front door open? He's lost now!" Konidaris speaks of the "sickening feeling" that "washed over" him and the sense of blame and later resentment. Moreover, beyond this one memorable moment, he talks of being "consumed by a self-imposed sense of responsibility for [his] brother's safety and well-being." One year younger than his brother, he took on tasks that transformed him into a caretaker and teacher. Before his brother was toilet trained, Konidaris cleaned up after him; he comforted him in new surroundings, translated his distinctive speech, assisted in speech therapy, and strove to prevent his self-abuse. Once, when his brother began an especially aggressive "biting fit," he "instinctively shot [his] own wrist into [his] brother's mouth." Caught between trying to stop his brother by taking the pain himself and testing just how far he might carry his rage, Konidaris ended up finding a "newfound unspoken trust" with his sibling: "He did not bite me. The sweat and redness left his face, his breathing slowed to normal. He maintained eye contact with me the entire time—a rarity. I had done the unthinkable. I had penetrated his defenses and his irrationality with my own irrationality." I cannot help but see this arm thrust as an emblematic gesture.

But, I wonder, what kind of comfort comes from this absorbing all but the feel of teeth in the flesh? What other mark, then, gets left?

If Jason Konidaris had been the young man on the tower, what would we have seen? What would he have voiced? He might have said what James McNeil expresses at the end of the *Reader's Digest* article: "Yes, I've given [John] a lot...but he's given me more. He gives me unconditional love. Am I my brother's keeper? Absolutely."

After all, in the final thoughts of his own narrative, Konidaris echoes these sentiments: "I have gained infinitely from the relationship I have with my brother. To him, I owe my character. I am a better person, a more complete person—one who achieves the daunting feat of balancing compassion, discipline, and understanding." But a full listening resists this half-story, this quarter-truth. Attend closely to what prefaces and then concludes the commonplace, seemingly clichéd script of the hero's tale and its deeply-felt confession of unconditional love:

> I have been labeled Sibling of an Autistic Individual. With this label come the highs and lows of a dozen lifetimes. I receive little or no feedback or thanks from the target of my endless efforts—my brother. I speak for a majority of siblings when I say that we are self-motivating. We expect little in return for our efforts. When minor successes do emerge, they take their place as trophies on a shelf—highlights of our lives. We battle to maintain a normal lifestyle for ourselves, all the while bearing the responsibility that few normal siblings could comprehend. We are not martyrs…. My infinite patience is matched only by my ever-present cynicism.

Should we see these reflections of the sibling life as contradictory, as a confused mix of pride and resentment, the signs of a desperate and compassionate gesture, an extended arm toughened by the threat of bite marks? Perhaps. But such a confession may not reveal a contradiction at all. It may simply be a glimpse of the complex middle place of a more complete tale.

Then there is Sarah, eighteen at this writing, entering into the various stories that she hears and sees and imagines from the expanding panorama of memory. She, too, has offered a version of her life with Jacob, later narrated in a February 13, 2007 *Kalamazoo Gazette* profile of our family entitled "Autistic Teen 'Lives in His Own World.'"

After taking the time to observe Jacob at Special Olympics basketball and bowling, interview Mary and me, and join our family's 6:30 am, pre-school routine, the writer, Linda Mah, later spent an hour listening to Sarah. "She sees her brother as pretty happy," Mah writes. "His life is filled with interests such as music and movies—in particular, Disney films. His obsession with movies results in what Sarah calls 'dialoguing,' during which Jacob replays dialogue from his favorite films to help express himself." In the section "How his sister copes," Sarah speaks of Jacob's obsessions, his listening endlessly to a cassette so that "you find a 'Sesame Street' song has been burned into your brain for the rest of the day." She tells of the meltdown at the library: "This time was different….I got mad at him. I remember hitting him back. I blamed him for his autism." And then she switches back to the reality of the ongoing desire to understand and accept her brother, how "it's hard to hold a grudge": "He's funny and goofy. He'll get in your face and say, 'Laughing alert!' Sometimes he's infectiously happy. Sometimes he's obnoxiously happy. He just wants you to be happy." In these words, I hear the richness of her experience; I know someone has listened, someone who did not come with their own story to tell.

But Sarah did not speak of the deep sadness that comes when she thinks of her friends and their siblings. She did not say how she often plays with their younger brothers and sisters, how she returns home and tells of conversations with them, how she unknowingly intones the desire for a home language not inflected with the un-spoken vocabulary of taking care of rather than spending time with Jacob. She did not say that when Mary and I fall asleep by 10 pm at night, when she is home, she cannot sit up with Jacob and watch a movie or order a pizza and pick it up with him, driving together in the dark streets like thieves, cranking up the radio as the hot slices steam the window. And it was Mary who had to remind me that it was Sarah who taught Jacob how to say, "I love you." And it was me who told Linda Mah so that it could become part of the story: "A few years ago Sarah taught Jacob to say "I love you, too" by forcing him to say it to her every time she left a room. She told him, "Jacob, this is what you have to do when someone says, 'I love you,'" their father said. 'Does he know what it means? Does it matter? Jacob is saying it when we say it. After a while it becomes something."

It is becoming something with each telling. It is always

becoming. After all, I know now what I could not express out of my despair then: to supply the words is to provide the meaning.

At the end of this past summer, after returning home from a writer's conference, I stepped on to our back deck and registered an absence on the landscape. And then, quickly, I saw what was no longer rising from our neighbor's yard: the green tower. The only sign of the old windmill frame emerged in worn places in the grass, peony bushes forming a square, and the ivy growing between the concrete footings. Owing to another storm that had collapsed two cedars along their back fence line and the loss of the tower, we can now see a greater expanse of land to the east, feeling for the first time the flow of the hill down toward the family housing apartments of Western Michigan University and, even further, the line of thick trees that form the boundaries of distant neighborhoods. This taking down of the tower and the opening up of the landscape is not a metaphor or a sign of past or passing things. But I can understand the hopeful pull toward such a reading.

On some weekends, Sarah comes home from college, sleeps until late morning, straightens her hair, watches seasons of *Grey's Anatomy* on DVD, and, if Jacob begins to show signs of frustration or aggression in the transitions of early evening, accepts the wisdom of leaving for a time. It seems she has begun to see that Jacob's obsessions signal what he, too, laments. They are accommodating their different ways of knowing, adjustments and understandings that demand the deciphering code of shared memories and the vocabulary of hundreds of movies, videos, and songs. On occasion, Sarah will sing "We're a duo, a DUO!"—and, perhaps, Jacob will join her.

Once, on the way to visit Sarah in Ann Arbor after her knee surgery, Jacob realized that he had left print-outs of "FAVORITE DISNEY CHARACTERS" and his list of "DOG FRIENDS FOR GYPSY" at home, two pages that he had worked on the day before and planned to have with him during the drive. In his frustration, he said, "I will hit Sarah. I will hit her." For miles we rode out his effort to deal with his own loss and worried what would happen when we arrived. But, when Sarah came out from her dormitory, swinging between her crutches, he spontaneously jumped out of the car, saying, "I must help my sister." In the February wind, he put his arms around her shoulders and pressed his nose to her cheek.

No one saw this moment but us. But it is possible to retell it now, to see the float of Sarah's hair and Jacob's hands holding one crutch. He is thinking that he is keeping her from falling—and, from our angle, he is. Before we open the car door to take them in, they lean against each other until they find a kind of balance. For a moment, we worry that they may stumble, that Sarah might twist her swollen and tender knee, but that is not what happens at all. We hold the car door open, uncaring of the cold air rushing in and the fear of losing one of Jacob's papers to the wind. "I love you, too, Jacob," Sarah finally says, amid her brother's wordless gestures, before letting him bring her to the car.

IV. Artifacts

FALLEN FRUIT

CLUTTER

AN ARCHAEOLOGY OF YEARNING

FALLEN FRUIT

*My house is a museum of sorts, cluttered with countless pages of my
son's scattered and unframed art. On busy weeks, Mary and I grow
weary and let the papers litter the flat spaces: the piano and organ
benches, the steps, the end tables, the kitchen counter, the bookshelves,
the dining room table, and, of course, the ample square footage of the
carpeted floor. The sketches are the steady harvest of my son's fertile
and repetitive imagination, the overripe fruit that burdened the limbs.*

*Just as the sheets continue to multiply, so have the numerous
bins to give them order. In one container, we sweep his lists—Dragon
Tales characters, the human voices behind favorite animated figures,
the names of the seemingly insignificant animators whose fingers have
carefully cropped and lined the margins in The Lion King. (When my
son was around six, he created a fifteen-foot scroll of one movie's credits, all the way to "Special Thanks To" and "The End.") In other bins, we
put his endless drawings of Bert and Ernie and Madeline. Some of the
characters are complete; others exist as limbs or faces or other beginnings. During these weeks, memories accrue like his drawings. We feel
their edges underfoot, trespassing onto the last of the empty spaces. At
times, when our wonder has been worn away, we push them aside in
panic or indifference.*

*On occasion, I think far out into the future and imagine that our
house has become an abandoned place, a site where scattered drawings
are the only signs of the artist. I recall an empty farmhouse that had
been surrounded by new homes on the west side of Storm Lake; its windows were tall and narrow and the curtains inside had begun to decay*

to reveal furniture, old mirrors, and wood crates. In the small towns and old farm groves of Iowa, these houses often remain for decades. Driving to and from college and on my way to Mary's farm, I passed such a place: a first generation homestead that had taken on the color of tree trunks and, at sunrise and sunset, collected the unbroken light shooting over corn tassels.

In the way that land takes in a sagging porch, I know this place. I know how to find the foundation long after the walls have fallen in and fires have reduced rafters, roof boards, and shingles to ash. I can drive by unknown groves now and see how the trees make room for all that seems lost. If I stop and climb the fence, not worrying of how I might look to others cruising by or whether a farmer might stop and question my pausing, I can find where the lane ran, the fireplace brick rose, and the cistern collected the rain. I have done this. It is amazing how much can be remade if one does not fear the tall grass and hidden nail, the splinter or fragment, the disorder in what has fallen, the momentary gap between things.

CLUTTER

When I was in grade school, I helped my mother with her upholstering business. On summer mornings (or on an occasional Saturday during the school year), I was dropped off at her room on the west end of my father's cement block auto body shop. Once there, I pulled staples or tacks from worn furniture. It was tedious work that sometimes bloodied the fingertips. If a chair or couch were old and made of hard wood, the staples would often break when I tried to pry them up with a straightedge screwdriver. To get out the two small spikes, I had to grab pliers, grip, and pull. When not accompanied by one of my two sisters, I felt the loneliness of the labor, taking occasional breaks to wander among the rolls of fabric along the wall or climb narrow makeshift steps to a small attic. Beneath the dim light of a hanging bulb, I marveled at an old crank phonograph. When I tired of the attic, I explored the things gathering dust near furniture: the nickelodeon jukebox, colorful fabric samples, the 78-speed records, thick and heavy, leaning in an old box. I kept seeking the things that came up through the mess, the partial newspapers or magazines with dates from before I was born, 1950s calendars with women in one-piece swimming suits and cars with wings for quarter panels.

I am still a wanderer in that backroom. I have replaced the real things with words on a computer screen, legal pads, the backs of receipts, church offering envelopes, and blank margins of newspapers. With their imperfections and overuse, I have come to see that even common things from the past carry enough clues. In the worn chair, the beauty is just above where the wood bone breaks through the finish; the pale blemish speaks of the nervous or animated hand sanding the curved arm of the furniture in the rhythm of worry or conversation. And, if I follow the forearm past the elbow, I may find myself looking into my mother's or father's face, glimpsing the features of a smile or frown elicited from what might have been their own remembering.

I have learned to start with just the thing itself, knowing that the artifact may be enough to sketch out the emotional grid. And so now the inventories of past places clutter my own rooms, awaiting future work and wandering. But now I go into memory with different purposes: to share a place of longing, to bear witness to desire without getting stuck in mourning what has passed and anticipating anxiously what will come. I want to understand loss as a mystery working its way through layers of soil, a seed that grows deeper and higher with the proper tending.

Let me finger through the slips of paper and see what comes forth from the clutter. For the moment, let me push away Jacob's artwork, grade school schedules, and Challenger Little League certificates. Let me set aside Sarah's college letters, soccer team pictures, and Amtrak ticket stubs from a trip to Chicago. I want to wander away to the places that I had lost in the years of surviving. I think that they will lead me somewhere that I need to go.

Here is a scrap of words scribbled in a notebook, a description of an old radio that fits on my parent's nightstand at 919 Pinecrest Drive in Storm Lake. The fragment calls out a series of colors, shapes, and sounds. Beige. Soft cloth over a speaker trembling with the bass. Rectangular. The dial, round, on the right front, the size of a coaster. The radio looks like a miniature stereo console, the kind from the 1960s with speakers on the left and right, the turntable in the middle under a lift-up lid. A song plays. The Lettermen's "Can't Take my Eyes Off of You."

Suddenly, I am at a bedroom doorway, watching my mother listening intently. I am in my pajamas. She looks up. She tells me that she likes this song and then turns inward again to listen. I can not be more than nine years old, in third grade. In the right corner of the room, near the wall, a glass lamp glows in the corner. On my left, opposite the light, the closet door is slightly open, a column of shadow cuts up the space. Outside, beyond the open window, the late spring lilac bushes, a few purple sprigs hanging in clusters, mingle their sweet aroma in the air as they catch the last of the dusk light.

What is in this moment that must be remembered? How can something so small, as seemingly inconsequential as a hesitation in breath or stride, persist so evocatively in my mind? What right combination of things passed down the moment like a fossil shell in stone, like a handprint on a cave wall? Now I know that I cannot understand her or myself without this memory, this lingering lyric, traveling under the crease of the open window, mixing with the last of the lilac scent and the damp of the early evenings of late spring, settling like a seed in some tended space. Her need to hear something so fleeting, to let music take her back to herself, broke the order of things, left an artifact of desire. What would it mean to live without these moments, to have cultivated a self with only the limited vocabulary of self-denial? What does it mean to be a witness to and for the things that leave such a mark?

Another scrap of words. A pair of worn figure skates. My father's. Black. Shoelaces frayed at the ends. To fit the worn thread through the holes the skater needed to put the tips in his mouth, smooth the strands to a point with spit, and then finish the lacing. The leather swells at the ankle. Dust polishes the heel; wisps of cobwebs float between sole and blade. Then this memory: watching my father ice skate on a Sunday afternoon.

We stopped the car on the west side of Storm Lake, across from the water plant where the snow had not yet drifted in ridges on the frozen water. My father left the rest of us along the shore scrambling to lace up our own skates—or at least I seem to remember the cold beneath my thighs while I paused to watch my father skate. He circled the ice, relaxing in the way a bird releases its wings to the wind, letting his body glide with each lean and push. He grinned like a boy, and, when he dropped his arms to his side and settled into a rhythm, I saw the same distant gaze that slid across my mother's face.

Once I wore my father's skates to play hockey and learned why hockey players do not wear figure skates. I was in eighth grade and, along with friends, had become enamored of the occasional game televised on Saturday afternoon. On the south shore of the lake, a friend and his father had cleared snow from the surface, drilled holes to bring up water to smooth and freeze the make-shift rink. For one winter, we made room for hockey between basketball practices and games. My father's figure skates had a jagged front edge and a long, sharp end; both features were not desirable in a game involving rough checking among amateur skaters. (Only one of my friends had begun to acquire the skill of skating backwards.) Near the end of a four-on-four game, I was checked off the cleared ice, rolling over one or two times before getting back up and looking for the culprit. When I sat in my friend's basement after the game, pulling off the layers of socks, long underwear, jeans, and snow pants, I noticed a large bloody splotch on the inside of my left calf. I had jabbed out a sizable piece of flesh with the end of my right skate. I still have the scar, round and milky white.

Not long after we had moved an hour and a half north to Spirit Lake, Iowa, I wore my father's skates one last time. I was home during my sophomore year at college and found them in the basement. By this time, my feet had grown to a size twelve, and, unlike earlier years when I wore thick pairs of insulated socks, I could only squeeze into the skates with thin tube socks. It was a rare early winter; the lake had long frozen solid, but no snow had fallen to mar the ice with drifts or a rough mixture of snow-laced ridges. Without the snow, the ground soaked up the noon sun, enough so that the air temperature could rise to near freezing. I carried the worn, dull blades down to the shore, slipped off my boots, and, sitting on a section of dock piled near the sand, laced up the skates.

In a lifetime, a day such as this might come just once: a warming sun and snowless Iowan landscape in late December, blue sky, shore cluttered with the convenient furniture of docks and boat slips, grass wisps barely catching a suggestion of wind, a vast tray of frozen water, no sound but the scraping and quiet sliding of blades. I could not stop grinning, could not stop the rhythmic motion that carried me much too far down the shore. On the way back, I had to stop and rest. I bent over, hoping to peer through the ice; I was surprised that I could not. I had thought that it was water that I skated upon, not something else, something that had changed but not changed, a bruise-tinted mystery whose opaqueness melts into clarity only when the eyes close.

I write nearly thirty years distant from this solitary skating and then ten more from my father's shoreline. I tie the ends of the skate laces together and put the blades upon the shelf. I store them just beyond my reach, just far enough away to ask the muscles to flex and chest to lean into the body memory of fighting for balance before being carried home on the ice. But the skates are hard to keep on the shelf. They are like the artifacts that keep breaking their way to the surface, waiting to be named and understood.

In their own way, the blades are calling me back to myself, to layers broader or deeper than the clutter of recent years with Sarah and Jacob. And so the remnants of the past take up more and more room like magazines stacked upon an end table or overlapping along the bed's edge. But the more distant things mix with memories less easily framed, pages crimped for future attention and marked with false starts. If I am to witness, I have one more fragment to bring forth.

A black interview folder. Thin. Six plastic inner slips to hold single sheets of paper. A gift to Mary. The first page, on holiday stationery: "Christmas 1995 Kalamazoo." On the second, a typed poem, Liz Rosenberg's "Married Love." Opposite, on the facing sheet: "Itinerary: First...Breakfast and Coffee/Browsing: Barnes & Noble." The next page, Galway Kinnell's "After Making Love We Hear Footsteps." Another itinerary sheet inserted opposite: "8:00 am Bagels and Coffee, 9:00 am Unscheduled, 10:00 am Morning Movie." Three plastic slips empty. It is another artifact of desire, a gift to Mary after another fall of scrambling to balance work with the obligations of home.

Did I fulfill the contract of the gift? Did we find someone to spend the morning with Sarah, then five, beautiful and endlessly talking, and Jacob, approaching three, wordless, a wind-up whirl of energy? I think that we did not. I know that I did not.

Can I hold this thing and not wither in the self-talk of what might have been? Can I bring it out from the bottom of the drawer and accept it for its desire, the connecting pull of it, even with whatever frailty hurried its making?

At times, we must learn to impose seasons upon ceaseless things, upon the guilt that ever finds new soil or the regrets that take over untended gardens like moss and ivy. We must understand what distinguishes passion from desperation. It is the history of letting something end, or of letting go, of reading the artifacts and words as if they are another's as well as one's own. Sometimes it is enough to scribble something, file it away, and come back as a stranger with wonder and compassion and a willingness to offer a blessing like ash on the forehead. Sometimes the end seems in the nature of things. More often, the end comes at some naming or with some formal feeling: a candle lit and blown out after some prayer, a last refrain, a winter or spring offering left at the doorstep or bedside and then put away. It is this kind of remembering that will bring us out.

The things themselves, too, have their own mysterious completeness. They give clues as to how much more needs to be said and done. Next to my notes and essay drafts, Jacob's scattered drawings from the previous night, Sarah's hair iron, and a Christmas centerpiece, the black folder from over a decade ago lies open. I am reading the last stanza of Rosenberg's "Married Love;" I am typing it again for this moment, and then another reader's:

> I turn to you in the dark, O husband,
> watching your lit breath circle the pillow.
> Then you turn to me, throwing first one limb
> and then another over me, in the easy brotherly
> lust of marriage. I cling to you
> as if I were a burning ship and you
> could save me, as if I won't go sliding down
> beneath you soon, as if our lives are made of rise

and fall, and we could ride this out forever,
with longing's thunder rolling heavy in our arms.

I am not a breath of light or fire. Mary is not a burning ship. But I know the bed that holds Rosenberg's desire, the rise and the fall, the thunder that rumbles in the limbs, that leaves the arms shaking with the lift of the next new burden.

But, in working through this clutter, I discover more than regret. I find what to pick up and how to hold it in my hand: a daughter's hairbrush or soccer shoe, a children's book, a black folder, a *National Geographic*. I quicken to things that point to what has been, to artifacts that frame how stories can be told. They can be scraps of paper that grid out yearnings into flesh and blood. They can be anything, almost anything.

AN ARCHAEOLOGY OF YEARNING

Before we moved from our previous home in the spring of 1997, Mary and I asked the real estate agent if we could arrange a final journey through the new house. We were learning to accommodate five-year-old Jacob's autism and had heard stories of children who did not easily adjust to a new home. For my son, a stable living space—a familiar shape and arrangement of rooms and an unchanging cycle of sun and shadow upon the walls—provided a predictable backdrop in a world of unpredictable people and their intrusive desires. Within this steady setting, the noise and motion of shifting human forms seemed less unsettling. So, holding a borrowed video camera, we entered our modest cape cod as if the living room were a lunar landscape. In our old brick house, the rental property of my college employer, Jacob would pull down the shades, watch videos flicker like strobe lights on our darkened walls, and line magnetic letters in hieroglyphic script on the wood floors. Looking through the frame of the camera lens at the new space, I tried to imagine how my son would see the cream-colored carpet, the narrow kitchen and flat white cabinets, and the sharp angles of his bedroom ceiling. Would the texture of his past find passage to this future life? Could his way of seeing the world find accommodation here? And, importantly, how might we know?

As it turned out, my son fell in love with the back deck and, as a result, embraced what he soon came to call the "white" house. We realized, given his dancing and theatrical miming, that he saw the deck as a longed-for stage where he could perform the script of his interior world. In the first weeks after our move, he entertained Sarah, Mary, and me with the rituals of this inner drama. In his silent movements, we picked out segments of various scenes from Winnie-the-Pooh and Disney videos and thus the context if not the meanings of his play.

Within the first weeks, he made the space his own. One mark has weathered the sun, rain, and snow of over a decade-long residence: a thickly-chalked "The End" on the concrete block of the back foundation. In their own way, these words turned the new space into something familiar, for they represented an ongoing interest. When Jacob was between the ages of three and four, we noticed his fascination with the scrolling credits at the end of movies and then his attempts to gather magnet letters into corresponding word-shapes on the floor. In what first appeared to be random groupings of letters, we began to discern "Sing-Along Songs" or "Walt Disney" and then "The End." In those years, he would use his own spit to draw the words on house or car windows or find a stick to dig out the letters in dirt. Even now he continues to write "The End" in the sand of Lake Michigan beaches, on the steamed-over mirror of our medicine cabinet, and, occasionally, on the white paper that clutters the former playroom. Such persistence marks autism's "restricted repetitive and stereotyped patterns of behavior, interests, and activities," fixations that manifest themselves in such things as "apparently compulsive adherence to specific nonfunctional routines or rituals." Though useful in providing diagnostic criteria, however, this definition from the fourth edition of *The Diagnostic and Statistical Manual of Mental Disorders* or *DSM-IV* seems incomplete, unable to capture the essence of my son and the desires that motivate him. In the ofttimes wearying repetitions of Jacob's routines arise the art and spirit of his vital being, a consciousness that yearns to meet across my own habits of knowing.

A few years after we had settled into the house, I ran across an August 2001 *National Geographic* article with photographs of the stunning thirty-thousand-year-old art from the Chauvet-Pont-d'Arc cave in France. By this time, we had already begun archiving Jacob's endless drawings of storybook, movie, and television characters. In fact, I had picked up the magazine just after sorting nearly a ream of Poohs, Madelines, Berts, and Big Birds in various stages of completion. His portfolio offered evidence of an ability to employ sophisticated perspectives and fine detail that defied typical developmental models. In short, he was not drawing as any nine-year-old should draw.

Even before he began to develop dexterity with his fingers and sketch with precision and control, Mary and I noticed how shapes and colors held his attention and compelled him to respond vehemently to the errors of our own drawings. As early as three, we understood that he wanted us to draw the Walt Disney emblem that opened many videos. At first, he accepted our rendering of the image, but, as we began to color the wording with magic markers, he grew frustrated, cried, and tantrumed uncontrollably. In a later attempt, Jacob finally took it upon himself to hand us one marker at a time, signaling his desire to have single colors shade particular sections from left to right. When we viewed a video at some later point, we realized that the Disney emblem served as a kind of color check; for a few seconds in the video's opening sequence, the primary colors passed from left to right, forming a kind of moving rainbow. Jacob's deeply-felt frustration came out of his inability to describe in words what he wanted and our blindness to the full dimension of his desire. We literally did not see the shifting colors and the animated designs that textured his imagination.

Mastering the use of crayon, pen, and marker, then, became essential to Jacob, for he could not count on others to render in color, shape, and perspective what was so crucial to his world. He came to prefer the fine lines of ink pens and began to produce a multitude of characters. The drawings grew from rough copies of book images to xerox-quality reproductions—so much so that others often asked whether the drawings were traced. As time passed, Jacob could not keep apart the worlds of Winnie-the-Pooh, Sesame

Street, and Madeline. With an ever-increasing population competing for the stage of his eight-and-a-half-by-eleven-inch canvas, Jacob's drawings began to show visual depth and perspective. Bert and Ernie stood before the taller and broader figures of Cookie Monster and Big Bird. Often, Elmo or Oscar the Grouch were turned away from the viewer or their bodies were just entering the page, as if hurrying in from off stage. In other drawings, he narrowed roads and rivers to suggest distance. (Typically, children between seven and eight draw figures all on the same visual plane, their bodies facing forward; they rarely use the whole page or create a sense of depth.) At eight, he drew the Disney castle, roughly doubling lines to suggest a three- not two-dimensional object. And, at times, he would start drawings in places that seemed entirely random and without any plan—with first the nose or arm or shoe—and fill in the whole character without any hesitation. If he did pause, his face and eyes seemed intent on viewing an inner image, one that could emerge whole no matter the starting place. Occasionally, he would carry these images to us and smile, as if proud; most often, the drawing seemed a way to find a calm space in the confusion of a busy day or a new environment. We learned to take his drawing things wherever we traveled. After a difficult six years following his diagnosis at three, his paper, markers, and pen enabled us to venture out to eat or to a movie. His art liberated us from the confines of our home.

In books of art fundamentals, teacher-artists talk of the "vocabu-lary of space": horizon line, interpenetration, and linear perspective. Jacob had the practice without the theory. In *Design through Dis-covery: An Introduction to Art and Design*, the text notes a concept that encompasses his capacity to create an illusion of space. "Intuitive space," it explains, "is independent of strict rules and formulae"; it is "not a system, but a product of the artist's instinct for manipulat-ing certain space-producing devices." Fundamental to this idea is the sense that an artist may first work from within, from some desire to give order, meaning, and emotion to space, and that this yearn-ing precedes technical skill. Perhaps it is this desire that draws the layperson to art. While lacking a learned vocabulary in interpret-ing realistic or abstract paintings, watercolor or charcoal, clay or ce-ramic, the uninitiated viewer senses some intersection between their own interior landscapes and the artist's inner vision. The artist and spectator share the desire for expression; their yearning is a point of contact.

That, as a father of a child with autism, I should sort through reams of scattered paper with such dedication conveys more than desperation. It embodies all the unsettling dimensions of love: a yearning inflected with hope and faith, a disciplined belief in mys-tery, the obligation of attending to common things. In one picture that Jacob tossed indifferently on the floor, for instance, Madeline and Miss Clavel, the nun who serves as her teacher and surrogate mother, sit on a river bank facing a sunset, arms around the other's waist and backs to the front of the page. Effortlessly, in their posi-tions and postures, he had captured a moment of calm but in a way that seemed to keep the spectator at a distance. On another occasion, at my parents' home in northwest Iowa, he spotted a four-by-eight-foot piece of sheet rock leaning against the basement wall. With col-ored markers, he drew in Bert, Ernie, and Big Bird at first curious poses—and then filled in an apartment building background. Watch-ing the "canvas" take shape, I felt a quickening to the inner world that guided his vision when I suddenly realized that Bert's forearms were originally positioned to rest against a windowsill before the sill was there. Through his method, I glimpsed a mind that reveled in this safe and exciting world—Sesame Street characters waving from windows, looking upon an imagined thoroughfare vital and non-threatening, and, of course, entirely void of human faces. Though Jacob struggled then and wrestles even now with the confusing array of emotions animating the expressions of Sarah, Mary, and me, he had discovered how the minimalist lines of television and storybook figures communicated a range of feelings for which he had some understanding but no words. Estranged, I felt oddly closer.

Observing the litter and splendor of the Charvet cave art, discoverers and specialists experienced their own estrangement. "For decades," expert Jean Clottes writes, "scholars had theorized that art had advanced in slow stages from primitive scratchings to lively, naturalistic renderings." Clottes refers to Charvet's vast cavern of elaborate wall drawings: panels of palm prints, charcoal renderings of rhinoceroses, a leopard shaped and dotted with red iron oxide pigment, mammoths and bison whose forms follow the contours of cave walls. Specialists in prehistoric cave art first expected the extensive drawings to be among the most recent manifestations of an evolving craft, perhaps around fifteen thousand years old: "Then carbon dates came in, and prehistorians reeled. Approximately twice as old as those in the more famous caves, Chauvet's images represented not the culmination of prehistoric art but its earliest known beginnings. A few thousand years after anatomically modern humans appeared in Europe, cave painting was as sophisticated as it would ever be."

Seeing these beautiful images from supposedly primitive hands seized my imagination, and I soon located the Cave of Charvet-Pont-d'Arc website that offers a virtual tour of the cave as well as information about its discovery and responses to the art. John Robinson, a sculptor from England, describes his initial visit: "The first large wall of red dots gives you a wonderful sense of communicating with the makers, especially as you can occasionally make out that the Dots have fingers. I then proceeded over a jumble of stalagmites and rocks into a recess. I entered a little chamber, I looked and found myself staring into the eyes of the most beautiful Bear. The red outline is pure and graceful. I turned and saw another red Bear. What a pair. How did the artist draw such wonders in such a confined space, and why?" Yes, how and why, I wondered. To enter the dark space of the cave would have required significant planning: the need to bring in a light source, red ochre, charcoal, and scraping stones to prepare the wall surface. (In some places, the artists removed the softer, putty-like surface to get to the white, underlying limestone; in one striking panel, someone traced the image of a thick-maned horse with markings that suggest a shedding winter coat.) It would have demanded much of body and mind: the willingness to venture into the deep caverns, the ability to discover and then negotiate the possibilities and limits of the medium, the need to enter the haunting darkness with a light source that could never outlast the inner vision. It would have been work that lingered in the nostrils and on the tongue: the smoke of the fire, the taste of the red ochre that, at times, was mixed in the mouth and sprayed to leave hand marks or color an animal figure.

In such a primitive studio, the litter and incompleteness of various images become as significant as any fully realized painting. Some charcoal images, for instance, overlay much older sketches; later artists scraped the surface to prepare for a new rendering of their world. On some walls, bison and horses are hurriedly sketched. (Was the torchlight fading? Were the images the start of another elaborate panel or simply a novice's effort to master the conventions of form and medium?) In the four hundred and twenty animal figures marking the numerous caverns, the cave art reflects knowledge of representational conventions (e.g., the double arc of a rhinoceros ear) as well as improvisation (e.g., the use of uneven cave surfaces to embody movement and form). The roughness brings to light how the artists inhabited real and intuitive space. These ancient figures come alive through hurry and hesitation, through the juxtaposition of the done and undone, through the discarded, the flecks of charcoal on the cave floor.

Attending to the vitality of the images gives way to different kinds of yearning—the desire to know more of those who ventured into these spaces, to discover how these artists developed the means to communicate such a vivid interaction with their world. What do these beautiful renderings tell us of the mind of the artist? Can we enter the cave and recover their desires? Can our knowing ever move beyond the limits of our own minds in this present chain of time and space?

I have my own caves to enter. Looking upon my son as he lies in his bed gazing through me, I often find myself disheartened by what I cannot know of his world. In our bedtime ritual, I rest for a few minutes beside him and try to coax out his rendering of some experience of the day.

"Jacob, what did you do today?"

Silence.

"Jacob, what did you do today? 'Dad, I . . . .'"

My sentence template prompts a reply. "Dad, I…did computer."

"What did you do on the computer?"

This night, as on many others, he disregards my question and launches into a new interest. "We will watch *Home on the Range* at Monday Night at the Movies in June. I will invite Cecilia Latiolais and Chris Latiolais and Laura Latiolais, and I will say, 'We're here to do a Monday night movie for you,/About things we know how to do,/We're very glad that you have come,/So welcome, welcome everyone!'" I listen, unwilling to cut off the odd mix of fantasy and hope. In this new fascination, Jacob voices his desire to have the city of Kalamazoo show the animated film, *Home on the Range*, during their "Monday Night at the Movies" series. (Having transformed an asphalt parking lot into a park with bandstand and play area some years ago, the city had for a time introduced monthly outdoor movies.) For weeks, he has spent time developing a script for special invitations and creating tickets to hand out to the growing list (over fifty) of desired guests. At one point, he had coerced Mary into writing down the endless introduction and commentary. I also was compelled to spend a Saturday helping him make movie tickets. (More specifically, he had created the tickets; I simply found a way to print them back to back—and in color.)

During the day, he spends time on the computer typing up invitations to the expanding list of old friends and new acquaintances. While his later letters have evolved into a more hurried cutting and pasting of stock, favorite phrases, the initial writings are perplexing in their odd syntax and seemingly random inclusion of Seuss and Disney references. To the Latiolais family, he follows the opening salutation with:

> I will give you ticket number one for you. All of the people will get in line let me say the story of *The Lorax*:

>> I rushed 'cross the room, and in no time at all,
>> I built a radio phone. I put in a quick call.
>> I called all my brothers and uncles and aunts
>> and I said, "Listen here! Here's a wonderful chance
>> for the whole Once-ler Family to get mighty rich!
>> Get over here fast! Take the road to North Nitch.
>> Turn left at Weehawken. Sharp right at South Stitch."

> I'll say here's your ticket and Chris, Laura and Cecilia will say "Thank You, Jacob"

And then concludes:

> We will eat popcorn, pop and candy at the movies tonight On Monday June 13 on summer vacation let me say about *The Lorax* let's do all about the story about *The Lorax* again:

>> And, in no time at all, in the factory I built,
>> The whole Once-ler Family was working full tilt.
>> We were all knitting Thneeds just as busy as bees
>> to the sound of the chopping of Truffula Trees
>> Then . . . Oh! Baby! Oh! How my business did grow!
>> Now, chopping trees one at a time was too slow.

> People do all about movies like *Finding Nemo* and *Shrek* And I don't know something all about movies they should do all about movies like Disney's Home On The Range at Monday Night Movies, they will do all about tickets for anyone and me and you. Anyone can see all about things and anybody come and play for all of us to do all kinds of tricks for everyone
>> Sincerely,
>> Jacob Mills!

Though his words sometimes clutter rather than clarify, Jacob does not choose his storybook or video talk randomly. As a visual thinker, he often borrows "chunks" of language from Seuss or Pooh or various films because the scripts communicate some feeling, even if the words are not related to his specific situation. In many ways, language can be like color on a painting: words are the reds that convey worry or uneasiness or the blues that communicate calm or subdued emotions. Speaking to the non-autistic world, Jacob knows that language becomes necessary and so he uses it to translate a particular emotion (an anxiety or comfort or excitement). When much younger, for example, he first watched Dr. Seuss's *Cat in the Hat* with great difficulty, often leaving the room and indirectly viewing the video through its reflections on the living room windows. The video was a moving, shifting canvas with a texture that included both sound and color. Soon, at moments of excitement, we realized that he would say, "Cat in the Hat" and then only "Cat." In our private dictionary, "Cat" became a synonym for "overly excited" or marked moments of over-stimulation. Around the same time, when a friend came over to baby sit, Jacob became anxious that Mary and I would be leaving and stated, "Something doesn't smell right," a worry-filled exclamation that he borrowed from the lost dog, Shadow, in the Disney film, *Homeward Bound*. In both instances, the verbal depends upon the visual, but even then, the translation between the eye and ear is not literal. Mary, Sarah, and I had to experience Jacob's world without language, in his own visual terms; we had to think in pictures and first assume that enigmatic, seemingly random references to storybooks and movies might be intentional. We began to experience words as analogous to colors, as gestures in tone and shading, as the sound stroke that gave texture to the canvas of a discrete communication. But, just as learning this new "language" created the world anew in giving new names and images to things, it led to unsettling questions. To what degree did Jacob's striving to communicate something of his world underscore an aloneness and desire to be better understood? To what extent were his images and video talk manifestations of his yearning to connect rather than signs of isolation and difference?

2004

In *Thinking in Pictures*, Temple Grandin begins her first chapter on visual thinking by illuminating this relationship between the pictorial and the verbal: "I think in pictures. Words are like a second language to me. I translate both spoken and written words into full-color movies, complete with sound, which run like a VCR tape in my head." As an equipment designer for the livestock industry, she emphasizes the extraordinary usefulness of her ability to "archive" various images and later salvage them in her designs. She explains: "I create new images all the time by taking many little parts of images I have in the video library of my imagination and piecing them together.... To create new designs, I retrieve bits and pieces from my memory and combine them into a new whole." Significantly, Grandin also describes the necessity of finding visual symbols for abstract concepts such as peace or honesty, symbols that served her in understanding other people and in gaining a greater sense of her own way of knowing. Words suggesting abstract ideas or complicated emotions were meaningless without some concrete symbol or image.

The evolution of Grandin's ability to emerge from her isolation and connect with others, in part, is traced in her memoir, *Emergence: Labeled Autistic*. Not long after Grandin discovers and begins to use doors as the object-symbol through which to understand herself and her relationship to others, the book includes a letter from her mother that was apparently prompted by an exchange about the kinds of abstract ideas that puzzled the daughter. "You know," her mother writes, "I was thinking about our conversation on love and wondering how one would put down on paper what love is. It seems to me that love is wanting to make things grow and having a stage in their growth. First, one wants to grow oneself and one develops symbols in order to do this." Through both her ongoing study of and intimate relationship to the patterns of Temple's life, she discerns the profound importance of her daughter's fixations, but she also warns her not to get stuck on tangible objects at the cost of discounting or simplifying the intangible things such as empathy and desire that they symbolize: "Here's the difference. Human beings are alive and respond. Objects cannot speak to you or hug you. Objects are only something made out of imagination and energy and raw materials. They can only mean whatever meaning we give them. A human isn't a private symbol or a representation of our effort, but a living creature who answers us. We may not always like the answer. It may be different from what we expect, but this answering creature has a soul—a soul struggling to perfect itself just as ours is.... You and I each has our dream of perfection and in sharing of our dream we learn from the other."

So what am I to make of my son, this person with whom I share such intimate spaces and symbols? How should I understand the unique constructions of Jacob's imagination, the ways in which he too takes in the pieces of this world—the imperfect surfaces and puzzling sounds—and filters them through the medium of his distinct personality and consciousness? How can I move beyond the tendency to conceive of autism as limitation rather than another means of knowing? As characterized in the *DSM-IV* and other studies of autism, those with the impairment manifest "abnormal functioning" in a variety of areas, including "(1) social interaction, (2) language as used in social communication, or (3) symbolic or imaginative play." Termed the triad of impairments, professionals watch for behaviors in children manifesting developmental delays—or, differently put, psychologists and others are attentive to a child's indifference toward people through poor eye contact, lack or loss of language, seemingly nonfunctional routines, and unusual or repetitive play. In *Autism: Explaining the Enigma*, Uta Frith describes the last of the triad as a "severe impairment in the pursuit of imaginative activities with the substitution of repetitive behavior." In short, the imagination itself is depicted as atypical or dysfunctional.

Clearly, the tendency to "get stuck" lining up toy figures (as my son did with Sesame Street figures and stuffed animals), rewinding and viewing favorite scenes in videos, and endlessly watching movie credits can limit those with autism. Just how often can one hear a child demand all the new Burger King toys or Disney Sing-Along videos? (Curses upon those advertisements that urge people to "Collect them all!" and eBay for making it possible!) The more that I observe my son, however, the more I have come to believe that our unexamined notions of imagination limit us. It is true that Jacob's way of knowing did not display itself in play-acting human relationships and interactions with *Toy Story* or Sesame Street figures. Yet, in his remarkable ability to catalogue and "play" with images and in his manipulation of line and perspective when drawing Madeline's eyes and mouth, Jacob manifests a meaningful visual vocabulary. It is a creative language and practice emerging from a human impulse that he and I share: the yearning to meet in symbol.

Of course, some moments or meeting points are more poignant than others. In some instances, that is, we discern in painting or words or glances or fixations some urgent need to be understood or, perhaps, some burning desire to display the moving, inner vision of outer things. Once, some years ago now, I stumbled into one of these instances. Sorting through Jacob's drawings, I found one that depicted Madeline with nine "thought bubbles" extending from her head. The picture represented his attempt to answer my request to draw a dream that had troubled him. (Uncharacteristically, Jacob had tried to describe the dream to me in words before going to bed one evening.) In an effort to illustrate the episodic nature of the dream, the bubbles presented seven scenes: Madeline swimming under the sea with Genevieve (her dog), Madeline clutched by a teeth-baring rat king, Madeline sleeping, Madeline in an underwater ship, Madeline swinging, and, more cryptically, two bubbles depicting outstretched hands, extending upward, bodiless. Even now, studying this picture, I pick out more patterns: the recurring but varied way in which hands reach or clutch, the way that Jacob captured the weariness of the daydreaming Madeline with two short, simple lines above and below her right eye, the way that her dots for eyes directly meet the viewer's gaze at different angles of observation. How should I understand these disembodied arms, the weariness, this stare?

And what of Jacob's letter to our friends, the Latiolais? What am I to make of his insistent desire to be allowed to "say the story of The Lorax"? Seuss's book is a tale of how the initial, greed-driven chopping down of one Truffula Tree eventually results in the clearing of a whole forest. As a children's story, its Seussian language-play and the ultimate moral are not hard to understand. But what if I let the words become secondary and quicken my senses instead to a mix of shape, color, and sound? The emotional landscape bears even greater witness to regret and loss. In the end, the narrator and the Lorax remain the lone witnesses—except, of course, for the readers themselves. But am I letting my own doubt or desire intervene? It may be, after all, that the industriousness of the Once-ler family, the cars hurrying right at South Stitch and the disembodied hands busily knitting Thneeds, suggest something joyous, something to be understood in addition to the sense of loss that concludes the story. I wonder also at the way the chief Once-ler remains faceless, a fact that Jacob himself noted cryptically to my wife and me. "No face," he said. "No face."

And, I think, there is something more fundamental to be understood in the strange syntax and urgent appeal of Jacob's letter. In the letters and his own art, we witness his cavernous desire to give form to the deep-reaching spaces of his world. We linger at the entrance to this private place because we understand that the yearning is familiar and that, like air, such a pressing need finds release through even the narrowest of passages. To walk away or to dismiss what emerges from within is the ultimate transgression. In the end, Jacob asks for one simple thing—that, in becoming an audience to pictures flung upon a white screen, we bear witness through the lens of his knowing.

I wonder sometimes at my determined forgetfulness, my steadfast unwillingness to believe that these evening exchanges and strange obsessions demarcate impenetrable walls. Perhaps I have come to know that, in our stubborn routines, Jacob and I construct visual and verbal records, the bits and pieces to retrieve later in order to give meaning, create a bond, and find hope. In the accumulation of time and memory, we give visual or written form to our personal symbols and, whether intentionally or not, come to trust that these codes mark the possibility of connection. We meet in the ritual of these symbols. Thus, even as I visit and re-visit this endlessly transformative medium of language and form, I again recall my daughter's simple but intentional act of teaching Jacob to reply, "I love you, too" to our final "good night" and "I love you." It does not matter that Sarah had to give her brother the script. It can be enough that we meet in this familiar contour of sound, a place where the words themselves may simply signal an enduring presence.

In some crucial way, we may mistakenly believe that we must *literally* translate the symbols of another's presence into our own language or know in *exact* ways how another person comprehends the world—as if such translation and knowledge were simple and static or discoverable without our own unpredictable journeying. Is there not something that precedes this knowledge? Just how much, then, must we know of another and to what extent does the way we conceive of this knowledge impair and liberate us?

I think that there is no discovery without yearning, without the desire to find something ready for but eluding the eye and mind. Once, when I was my son's age, I watched a dried creek bed begin to fill again with water after a late August downpour. Upstream, the water had risen above the modest concrete dam and was winding to the lake at the stream's end. This creek was one of my favorite places. Near our family's seasonal, working-class cabin and beyond the edge of tall itch weed, the creek was never wider than six feet. It alternated between sand, rock, and mud bottom and held all that a young boy's imagination desired: minnows, crawdads, and even a bison skull. After I had found the skull and other bones during one especially dry summer, I spent weekends along the stream, imagining that I was like those individuals who were digging up dinosaur bones on the high plains. In the dry months, the last of the water pooled where the creek bent quickly or where tree roots had forced the current to deepen the bottom. Minnows died and mosquitoes buzzed, and the moisture lingered in the damp and subtle stench of decay.

On this particular day, I dug trenches for the trickling water, fingered through rocks pushed up along the ever-changing edge of the creek, and searched the bone-shaped stones. As the water reached one turn, I spotted an arrowhead near my stick. I am not sure how it caught my eye in the mud and cloudy water, but I am sure that my yearning was a precondition for all that flooded my young mind after I held it in my palm. Was this the stone that killed the bison? Who made the arrowhead and had he walked where I now stood? And, for a moment, I allowed myself to imagine that, out of the infinite layers of leaf and mud and the intersection of curiosity and climate, I held something that had been cupped in the palm of a distant hand. I realize now that I had no other purpose but wonder. Even then, I think, I yearned for a larger world, a place where a tangible hand extended across time and space, where something with flesh and wholeness could be pieced together from remnants. I wanted something holy. I yearned a special kind of knowing.

When Jean-Marie Chauvet descended with his two friends into the cave that now bears his name, he might have been impelled by a similar curiosity. The general area had long been known and explored, but the rush of air from a small opening evoked the desire to look further inward. While he might have imagined the possibility of discovering ancient cave art, he could not have fully predicted the magnitude of this particular find. Perhaps this is another dimension of yearning, the sense that our passions inevitably demand that we become witnesses, i.e., people who have seen and must enable others to see as well. After having cleared the blocked entry to an obscure shaft, after leaving and wearily returning with needed equipment, and even after their discovery of the drawings, they still hesitated before something deeper, the sense that some burden descended upon them. As described in the website's "Discovery" section, Charvet and his friends "made more discoveries, and came out feeling not only dazzled and enchanted, but also somewhat anxious, realizing the heavy responsibility they now faced." Interestingly, their actions mirror how people often approach a holy site. Returning on the next Saturday (Christmas Eve), they protected the cave floor from a kind of defiling by covering their previous path and footprints with a plastic sheeting. In doing so, they "thus defined the path that would be sacrificed for all the passage of all who would follow." In other words, they kept holy the untouched reaches of the cave and offered the possibility of finding and more fully understanding the signs of previous visitors: a footprint in the dust, bones scattered by bears or human hands.

The reflections of those who descend into the cave and return to give witness to their experience communicate awe. Specialist in Australian rock art and former editor of *Antiquity*, Christopher Chippindale writes: "Most striking is the extraordinary technical skill of the artists, the varied ways they used varied techniques to shape their images, the confident simplicity with which they could express even a rhinoceros with all its strength and spirit in a single line. As was said years ago of European cave-art, 'This may be the childhood of art, but it is not the art of children.'" Margaret Conkey, a professor of anthropology who specializes in French prehistory and prehistoric art, both resists and accepts the wonder that might lead us away from understanding the makers: "Although I myself have been critical of the breathless awe with which we celebrate Paleolithic art—an awe that all too often sets aside any real engagement with the images as social and cultural productions, with their makers, and their contexts—these images at Chauvet are, in many ways, awesome. Above all, the visit made me reflect on our ever shifting, if not elusive understandings of the past, while, at the same time, participating in actively constructing a new and emergent relationship between who we are and who we were."

Yearning, then, requires a humble imagination, the need to dedicate all of our ways of knowing to discerning with discipline and keen sight the makers and the nature of their makings. Just as it is easy to succumb to the belief that difference signals the impossibility of full and meaningful connection, so too is it easy to submit to or accept mere proximity to mystery, to be satisfied with abandoning the hard journey and collecting artifacts that gesture toward distant places. Yearning, however, demands toil and participation. Awe, after all, cannot be the end. Inevitably and almost always, the end requires the giving up and reframing of original definitions and beliefs. Perhaps this is the thing that is most feared: an initial venturing into a place without the possibility of returning unchanged.

My son eludes me. And, no matter my delicate reasoning, I still panic at how little I may know him and how little he understands me. I observe, theorize, invent, and narrate in order to shoulder away his seeming indifference. I learn new codes, new definitions, new ways of thinking. I accept intimacy on his terms: the backward embraces, the denial of nighttime kisses. I sometimes utter guttural sounds that over the years have formed the vocabulary of our play. "Gah" evokes laughter, chasing, tickling; such behavior begins to look strange now that he is a teenager, taller than my wife, and nearly wearing my shoe size. I demand that he make my body whole, not a glance or a limb haunting the edges of his vision; I lead his mind to the reality of my hands and arms.

Jacob worries about death and weeps longingly for Mr. Hooper of Sesame Street. He refuses to believe that Mary or Sarah or I will leave as Mr. Hooper has left his friends. Within the past few years, he has developed an interest in calendars and maps. He is beginning to piece together his past with the mathematical logic of days, months, and years. He remembers former babysitters and teachers, books and videos from the shelves of homes visited long ago, times when we picked him up early from school for a special trip or event. He marks the calendar with Elliot's Hanukah Party (to assure that it will happen again in December). He knows the wandering highway lines of our trips to family in Iowa (the roads that wind past the southern tip of Lake Michigan) and laments Kalamazoo's West Main Avenue for its endless stoplights and unsettling delays in returning home from Meijer or Target.

I fear just how "normal" this has all become and yield to a need for the unfamiliar, to an awe that purifies this yearning, to a relationship to mystery that cultivates beauty from struggle and despair. I need this fullness to become who I was and can be. I need it to be vigilant, to endure change, to accept how the motion of other minds ultimately reminds me of my own strangeness and isolation.

On some nights, I awake as if in a cave and think of the future. Mary and I will exist as memories: a quick glimpse of arms reaching toward another's shoulders or face, an image of a hand upon a book, the scent of our bodies after the sweat of sleep, the tone of our young and old voices calling our daughter or son from distant rooms or down a stair. Our presence and wholeness will depend upon the imagination of those sorting through cupboards, files, and scrapbooks. Eventually, I arrive unwillingly on the image of my son, in some new home. No matter how much I have written or catalogued or kept in images, I know that the site of his life and mine will inevitably remain fragments and that only a visitor can bring us to life. I wonder then who the discoverers will be. How will their minds have been formed?

Before what will they have stood in awe? How far will they have ventured? How will they have played and imagined and encumbered themselves with mystery?

And, yes, I imagine a torchbearer, entering the cave of Charvet. In his hands, he holds charcoal or red ochre; in the stride, there is both awe and urgency, perhaps inspired by memory of a place where the wall curves to suggest a bison's chest or how a collage of palms might convey the form of a mammoth. As the sunlight dies outside, the artist mixes the red pigment with water or saliva and marks the wall. It grows dark this night, and, before he awakens from reverie to the reality of the dimming light of his fire, he sees in his mind's eye the sweep of muscles that tighten and arch a horse's neck, the curve of a bear's shoulder and flank. In his mouth, he tastes the red ochre that he had spit over his right hand. It is when he touches the dried pigment on the back of his hand and recalls the mark that he has left on the wall that he notices the last of the torchlight casting his everdimming shadow.

Even now, I can see him stumbling, then crawling within that deep place. It cannot be far, he thinks, to the cave's opening and the night air. At moments, he stops and weeps at what brought him into the utter darkness of that place. And yet, perhaps he does not weep; perhaps he finds his way out through the imagination of his hands, how the cavern lungs circulate air, how the dirt and stone too can be understood, how the red ochre paste still marks his path. Perhaps he discovers the hope that comes after you've lost your way.

Books from Etruscan Press

Etruscan Press Is Proud of Support Received From

Wilkes University

Youngstown State University

The Raymond John Wean Foundation

The Ohio Arts Council

The Stephen & Jeryl Oristaglio Foundation

The Nathalie & James Andrews Foundation

The National Endowment for the Arts

The Ruth H. Beecher Foundation

The Bates-Manzano Fund

The New Mexico Community Foundation

The Gratia Murphy Endowment

Founded in 2001 with a generous grant from the Oristaglio Foundation, Etruscan Press is a nonprofit cooperative of poets and writers working to produce and promote books that nurture the dialogue among genres, achieve a distinctive voice, and reshape the literary and cultural histories of which we are a part.

etruscan press
www.etruscanpress.org

Etruscan Press books may be ordered from

Consortium Book Sales and Distribution
800.283.3572
www.cbsd.com

Small Press Distribution
800.869.7553
www.spdbooks.org

Etruscan Press is a 501(c)(3) nonprofit organization.
Contributions to Etruscan Press are tax deductible
as allowed under applicable law.
For more information, a prospectus,
or to order one of our titles,
contact us at books@etruscanpress.org.